£1.99 Eco

48

Greece
on the Couch
session 1

By Mark Dragoumis

ATHENS ⁂ NEWS

Editor: Hilary J Teplitz
Designer: Yannis Smyrnis
Cover design: Angelos Tsakonas, Multimedia S.A.
Cover cartoon: David E Smith

The chapters of this book first appeared in the Athens News, Greece's English-language weekly newspaper, in 2001-2003.

ISBN 960–86395–5–7

Printed and bound in Athens, Greece by IRIS S.A.
Pre-press by Multimedia S.A.

Contents

IV) How the Greek 'nanny state' smothers university education

V) Prevalent corruption ensures there is always hope for the wicked

VI) Greek political parties struggling to differ

VII) And now for something completely different...

About the Author

MARK DRAGOUMIS, a Greek writer, former Eurocrat and government official, was born in Athens in November 1926. He studied Medicine at the universities of Geneva and Athens and began a post-graduate degree in Medical Sociology. He abandoned work on his thesis to join the movement against the junta that had taken over Greece on April 21, 1967.

He became involved in journalism and politics. He got a job first as a research assistant for Bedford College of London University and later as a research officer for the Tower Hamlets Social Services department. Upon the junta's collapse in July 1974, he was appointed head of the Press Office at the Greek Embassy in London, where he served until March 1982. He was subsequently posted as Press Counsellor to Warsaw, Poland. As an information officer of the Greek Government he put to use his command of languages and his knowledge of Greece's history, politics and culture.

In 1984, he left the Greek Press and Information Service and was appointed Head of the Greek Translation Department of the European Parliament in Luxembourg. In 1992, he returned to Athens to serve for three years, until his retirement, at the General Secretariat for Press and Information as Director of Foreign Services in charge of Press Offices around the world.

In 1991, he published – in Greek – a book under the title "Course towards Liberalism" (*Πορεία προς τον Φιλελευθερισμό*).

In 1995, he co-authored with Professor Thanos Veremis of Athens University the "Historical Dictionary of Greece", published by Scarecrow Press Inc. The same year, 1995 saw the publication of his booklet "Greece at War 1940-1945" in English and in Greek.

In 1998, he co-authored again with Prof. Veremis the work "Greece - Revised Edition", (volume 17 of the World Bibliographic Press), an annotated bibliography of books in English on Greece, published by Clio Press (Oxford, England).

Since 16 March 2001, when his first column was published, Mark Dragoumis has been a regular commentator of *Athens News.*

Acknowledgments

As the author of a book that strings together and classifies under seven chapters about one quarter of the commentaries I wrote for *Athens News*, I feel first and foremost beholden to the editor, Mr John Psaropoulos, who made this venture possible. Without his help and encouragement, none of the pieces at hand would have been written in the first place, let alone selected to appear in book form. I would also like to thank Ms Hilary Teplitz, who edited the book with the utmost care and saved me from many a false step.

I am also deeply indebted to those who helped me select them.

My friend Mr George Pagoulatos, Assistant Professor in the Department of International and European Economic Studies of the Athens University of Economics and Business (and a Rhodes scholar political scientist, holding an Oxford post-graduate degree, with many publications in English to his credit, of which a recent book on the Greek economy), has been a witty, stimulating, critical and generally helpful interlocutor in our continuous exchange of ideas on many political, economic and even philosophical issues touched upon in my weekly columns.

Another such, has been my son Philip – British-born, Oxford educated in the classics, London Business School post-graduate and now Athens-based financial analyst and consultant – who often helped me choose the right subjects at the right time and corrected me on a number of occasions.

I am also grateful to my friend and lawyer, Yannis Nikolaidis, of the law practice Nomiki Omada Athinon whose insights into the Greek "system" have been for me an eye-opener on many occasions.

I was amazed that the selections of the columns that should be included in the book made by all three were almost identical. The truth is all of them display a marked predilection for intellectual pursuits and a striving to understand the world around them.

My warmest feelings of gratitude go, however, to my wife, Lena Bali-Dragoumis, who has always found time in spite of her various professional architectural and town-planning commitments, to be the first reader, and stern critic, of anything I produce for publication. Her comments, ranging from the appreciative to the sarcastic, have been invaluable.

Greece
on the Couch
session 1

I) Who do the Greeks think they are?

REEKS or Hellenes? That is not the question. Delusional ideas about the "inalienable rights of Hellenism" are the question. Some Diaspora Greeks even display a syndrome that makes them think of themselves as the country's "ambassadors abroad", even if they are nothing of the kind, nor should they be. Interestingly, ideas of grandeur co-exist in Greece with an "underdog culture" that is now mercifully on the wane. Nonetheless, xenophobia is still rampant, having been solidly embedded in the school curriculum ever since Greece became a nation.

What, exactly, is in a name?

There is no meaning in the use of the 'H' word
(Hellenes) rather than the 'G' word (Greeks)

SOME years ago an American professor by the name of Samuel Huntington produced a theory about the clash of civilisations that would allegedly be a kind of continuation of the Cold War by other means. He opined that Christian Orthodox countries would never be able to practise democracy, capitalism and the rule of law. In 2000, the European Council decided to open its doors to help eastern European countries join the EU. They became full members in 2004.

This raises a more general question: Are democracy and capitalism teachable like mathematics, physics and medicine? An American journalist, Thomas Friedman, believes he has found new evidence that they are. "Greece", he wrote in an article published in the *New York Times* on 12 June 2001, "provides a wonderful laboratory for the most interesting clash going on around Europe today - the clash between two grand theories. One is Francis Fukuyama's notion that with the triumph of liberal democracy and free-market capitalism over all other systems, history has ended - in the sense that if your country wants to prosper, now there is only one road. And the other is Samuel Huntigton's "Clash of Civilisations" - the notion that culture matters in how, or whether, a country adopts capitalism or democracy, and that the religious fault lines of old will become the new fault lines of the post-cold-war era. I can report that Fukuyama is winning in Greece but Huntington is putting up a good fight".

As instances of the rear-guard action waged by the Huntingtonian old guard, Friedman mentioned, among others, the ID controversy, that was resolved a short time later. Chauvinism still needs watching in Greece but, fortunately, it is on the wane. Fifteen years ago an episode like the 2001 attack against the Greek Press Office in Skopje would have provoked a crisis of national hysteria. These days only a lunatic fringe works itself up into a transient fury.

Nonetheless, some foreign observers continue to bark up the wrong tree accusing the Greeks of delusions of grandeur in the use of their national name. There is no difference in the use of the "H" word (Hellenes) rather than the "G" word (Greeks). It is ludicrous to maintain that Hellenic Petroleum took its name because it suffers from an inferiority complex about the dull and monosyllabic "Greek". In modern Greek, Ellas is the country's name and *ellinikos* the only available adjective. Some "patriotic" Greek ignoramuses have suggested that the term "Greek" – used by foreigners – be banned because it was allegedly some sort of pejorative nickname introduced by the Romans.

"Greek", however, has impeccable credentials. Aristotle writes in his "Metereologika" (A.14) that in the territory around Dodona in Epirus and the river Acheloos, - believed then by some to be the cradle of the nation,- "there used to dwell those anciently called Greeks (Graikoi) but now Hellenes." Hesiod, an authority on genealogy, mythical or otherwise, mentions a hero named Greek (Graikos), son of Zeus and Pandora.

So, whether "Greeks" or "Hellenes", these people were pagan. The Orthodox Church in the Eastern Roman Empire (renamed Byzantium by Hieronymus Wolf in the 16th century) resented equally both these appellations. As a result, its faithful were simply called Romaioi (the Greek word for Romans) and their language Romaic. Contemporary Greeks still call themselves colloquially Romioi, using the term Romiossini as a collective noun. Should Hellenic Petroleum rename itself Petrelaio tis Romiossinis to please its Greekless foreign critics?

Delusional ideas can harm a nation's health

There are no such things as 'the inalienable rights of Hellenism', exactly as there are no such rights of Turkism, Bulgarism, Albanism or any other ethnic group in the area

HISTORY, in the sense of both a record of things past and events unfolding in the present, is full of ideas that fall into disrepute. Some, like communism and fascism – big, world-view visions - have needed war, mountains of corpses, untold human misery and a lot of time to be finally discarded. Others, more prosaic but still wrong and bad, vanish relatively unnoticed.

Who remembers, for instance, the "dependency theory" of underdevelopment that held "neo-colonialism" responsible for keeping third world countries poor on purpose so they could remain as reservoirs of raw materials and cheap labour for the advanced ones? It took the spectacular growth of the Asian "tigers" to put paid to such lucubrations. This is not the only case. Remember the "limits to growth" hysteria that predicted the world would run out of oil sometime during the last century? Remember the "indisputable" superiority of Japanese management, alleged to be uniquely capable of harnessing superior Asian values to modern business goals? Remember Keynesian recipes about "demand management" that led to hyper-inflation, the panacea of "incomes policies," or the panic over the alleged "population explosion"?

The truth is that some failed ideas and projects take a long time to die. Europe's "Common Agricultural Policy", for instance, continues to keep farmers living in the style they have been accustomed to, providing them with the wherewithal to produce goods too expensive to be sold, which are then collected by the Commission and dumped at ridiculously low prices on the world market. Any attempt to change the system generates furious anger in France (and in Greece) and so it goes on and on. Hopes that the EU's enlargement might put it out of its misery have not as yet materialised.

Bad ideas spreading out are nothing new, but those that gain instantaneous currency in our globalised world may be more difficult to combat, like those insidious viruses that invade our computers. Global terrorism, for instance, would not have been possible thirty years ago. A successful global response to it is still actively sought, but as the 9/11 outrage of 2001 becomes history and as the Iraqi conundrum continues, frustrated and impatient electorates may move their attention elsewhere.

There is one overarching delusional idea still endemic in Greece (but progressively losing its virulence) that needs to be uprooted before issues concerning Cyprus, the Greco-Turkish relations and the name to be given to the Former Yugoslav Republic of Macedonia start again to fester as they have done in the past. The Greeks must accept unreservedly, unequivocally, unconditionally that they are in no way superior beings deserving special treatment. There are no such things as "the inalienable rights of Hellenism" (*ta aparagrapta dikaia tou Ellinismou*), exactly as there are no such rights of Turkism, Bulgarism, Albanism or any other ethnic group in the area. Like everybody else, Greeks have human rights. That is all. The fact that they are not exceptional means they are not entitled to anything by hereditary right for what they are – or, rather, think themselves to be – only for what they do. The notion of the "chosen" people has never thrived in Greece except in the heads of some frustrated 19th century intellectuals.

Take two examples closely related to this form of Greek delusional thinking. If the claim of being the direct and only descendants of ancient Greeks - together perhaps with the odd, blue-eyed, God-forsaken mountain tribe in Afghanistan of alleged Macedonian ancestry - had simply led modern Greeks to try to emulate their alleged ancestors, no harm would have been done. But when such pretentious rhetoric was used as an argument to convince, for instance, the IOC to designate Athens for the next Olympiad, Greece simply looked ridiculous. It took the decisive, no-nonsense approach of a new team to bring the Olympics to Athens not because the modern Greeks are of ancient stock, but because they were able to prove that they could organise the Games safely and satisfactorily. They did so eventually, even with great delays and at an enormous cost.

The same goes for the Parthenon Marbles. The outbursts of the late Melina Mercouri about "our Marbles" generated condescending smiles and embarrassment all around. They allowed the Daily Telegraph to claim that the British were more genuine descendants of Pericles' values than the modern Greeks, just as Hitler maintained that the Aryan race in general, and the Germans in particular, were the "Greeks" of the 20th century. Now that Greece has abandoned such silly claims based on hereditary law and insisted that the Marbles be returned in order to restore the integrity of the Parthenon, her case has gained support. The only thing missing, as yet, is the promised new state-of-the-art Acropolis Museum to house them. If the British Museum were to give them back to Greece now, she would have to refuse the offer.

Perhaps the slogan of the new Greek government should be: Re-education! Re-education! Re-education!

Chauvinism, the last refuge of the ignoramus

Diaspora Greeks should not really believe that they are 'Greece's ambassadors abroad', according to the official rhetoric. They are not

DURING the bad old days when Andreas Papandreou used to enjoy playing the role of the "black sheep" in the EU, Greece was still asked to lead the Union when its turn came.

Those were "heroic" times when some Greeks at home and abroad felt proud and special, superior to everybody else while, at the same time, whining against imagined conspirators and wallowing in the "underdog culture" so vividly described by the European ombudsman, Professor Nikiforos Diamandouros, in his works.

Those were the days when a German politician was asked what he expected from the forthcoming Greek presidency, and replied icily that "it will be over in six months". Those were the days when Greece was not so much a European country in the Balkans but more of a Balkan country in Europe – more part of the problem than of any solution.

Those were the days of 1994, when Athens was (unsuccessfully) hauled before the European Court in the middle of its own presidency for imposing an idiotic economic embargo on the Former Yugoslav Republic of Macedonia (FYROM) in a flagrant violation of the principle of free trade.

Well, it seems that nostalgia for those "heroic" days still grips some. This columnist's view that Greece no longer needs "heroes" going ballistic at the mere mention of the word "compromise" provoked the ire of a reader, a Greek from Sydney Australia. The Slav Macedonians down under, he says, covet Greek territory, usurp Alexander the Great as their ancestor and claim anything "Macedonian" as theirs of right. "If you agree with Mr Dragoumis," he warns the editor, "then let these Slavs claim back all the above..."

Now, "these Slavs", as well as all Australians including those of Greek origin, can of course utter any inanity they like until they are blue in the face. They do not have the monopoly in the area to invent themselves a history, an ancestry and a "national ideology" bearing no relation to fact. After all, even the Gypsies residing in FYROM claim descent from the ancient Egyptians and honour the pharaohs as their forefathers.

In stark contrast, Skopje is acting sensibly - it makes no claims against Greece, welcomes Greek investors with open arms and relies heavily on Greece's diplomatic support. This was confirmed during a visit by George Papandreou, then Greek foreign minister, to all Balkan capitals, including Skopje in 2002, where he was lionised as someone able to pave their way to the EU sometime in the not too distant future.

Diaspora Greeks should not really believe that they are "Greece's ambassadors abroad", according to the official rhetoric. They are not. Many of them are so far behind developments that they would benefit greatly by keeping in touch with their Greek embassy on issues pertaining to Greece's foreign policy. The same would, of course, be true of Slav Macedonians... if only they had an embassy in Canberra.

As the *Economist* put it on 4 January 2003, FYROM "has no embassy in Australia because Greeks think the Former Yugoslav Republic that calls itself Macedonia has purloined the name from them, and the Greek vote counts for a lot in Australia. So as a sop to local Greeks... the Australian government has not yet allowed it to open an embassy in Canberra. The case of the missing embassy is an extreme but typical example of how diasporas have long exerted their influence."

There are FYROM diplomats in Athens and Greek diplomats in Skopje, but in Canberra only Greek diplomats are accredited. This is not the only example of diaspora chauvinism gone wild. In July 1998, a virulent letter-writing campaign organised and financed by Greek-Americans obliged Antonio Banderas, the actor, to renounce playing the part of Kemal Ataturk in a film planned by Tarquin Olivier, son of the famous actor Lawrence Olivier.

One such letter described Ataturk as "a savage maniac", a "paedophile" "a destroyer of Greek civilisation and, in general, a disgrace to human civilisation". Did the "patriot" who wrote such rubbish know that Eleftherios Venizelos, Greece's great statesman, proposed Ataturk for the Nobel Prize in 1934? Probably not.

However, not all diaspora Greeks espouse such armchair "heroics". An editorial in the *Greek American*, a weekly newspaper published in New York, said the intimidation campaign against Banderas had caused many Greeks "to cringe in embarrassment". Explaining its position, the editorial added: "All-out demonisation is not serious. The end result is to make us look like ethnic hysterics, with these groups' objections usually showing up our own chauvinism and narrow-mindedness more than anything else."

Diaspora Greeks should calm down. Their mother country - as well as their adoptive country and, indeed, the world at large - needs their skills, their business acumen, their contribution to culture, science and the arts. Not their drum-beating over conflicts past.

Dealing with immigration, the Isocratic way

The day a Hellenised Albanian visits Tirana and behaves like a Greek-American in Athens, Greeks will have embarked for good on assimilating the 'xenoi' who have come in recent years

GREEKS are not, as a rule, xenophobes, i.e. fearful of strangers. Unique among European languages, Greek uses the same word, *xenos*, to denote - since Homeric times - both the stranger and the guest. *Xenophilia*, or rather *philoxenia* - as the Greeks would have it - means hospitality, seen as a duty since ancient times. However, to many Greeks a *xenos* is a *xenos* and cannot pretend to be Greek.

In Modern Greece, various myths about racial purity, direct descent from the ancients and pretensions to exclusivity have sometimes generated suspicion, if not outright intolerance, against foreigners who take residence in the country. To start with, they call them names.

The Turks are collectively hated (although often liked on an individual level) and dismissed as *boudalades*, i.e. fat, stupid and uncouth. The Italians are *makaronades*, macaroni-eaters - a term of derision rather than hate, as its meaning developed during the failed attack by Mussolini against Greece in 1940. The Bulgarians are not called anything in particular. Instead, their very name can be used as an insult, as Professor Babiniotis noted in his dictionary some years ago. The collective word for Westerners in general is *koutofrangoi*, meaning stupid Franks, perhaps a remnant of the 13th-century occupation of Greece by brutish, iron-clad Frankish knights of the Fourth Crusade. The accusation of low intelligence, curiously, is also addressed to Americans. In Modern Greek slang a question referring to them bizarrely in the diminutive - "Do I look like a small American?" (*Moiazo gia Amerikanaki?* means, "Do I look like a fool?" The English, on the other hand, get a red-carpet treatment. They are called *lordoi* (lords) and are praised for their punctuality: *Egglezos stin ora tou* means, "Englishman in his time-keeping" or right on time. The word *tzentleman* (gentleman) is also a term of high praise. This columnist remembers a fisherman on the island of Poros speaking about a *poly tzentleman kyria*, i.e. a "very gentlemanly lady".

In the old days when Greece had a problem of emigration rather than immigration, such national stereotyping could be fun. Now, however, things have changed. Some 8-10 percent of Greece's population is made up of *xenoi*, and an increasing number of them wish to become Greeks (well, Greek citizens to start with). The issue has been on the agenda of EU summit meetings for some time, and plans have been afoot to promote a clearing-house of information on migration policies and programmes in which "best practices" from around the world could be identified and evaluated. Such an attitude is, of course, in line with the Thessaloniki EU summit in June 2003, which recommends in paragraph 28 of its conclusions "the elaboration of a comprehensive and multidimensional policy of integration of legally residing third-country nationals", adding that such a policy should cover among other areas "education and language training".

Immediately after the summit, the Greek education ministry, which has to deal with 10 percent immigrant children in Greek schools, revealed plans to set up special classes for them in 400 schools - besides the ones that are already multicultural.

There is also the imaginative project to establish The Athens Free School, a modern model school for immigrant and Gypsy children that will operate under the motto of a distich taken from a Greek folk song from the island of Patmos: "Holy Virgin, please bring cheer/ to foreign children coming here (*Παναγία μου παρηγόρα / Τα ξενάκια πού' ρθαν τώρα*)." The heart and soul of this project is Don Morgan Nielsen, a teacher at Athens College and educational innovator in the US, where he taught in programmes for Indian and Eskimo children. His ceaseless efforts to secure the finance, the building and the personnel for this innovative school have caught the attention of President Costis Stephanopoulos and Athens Mayor Dora Bakoyianni, among others.

What such laudable efforts will require, however, is a change in the prevailing concept of "Greekness". Modern Greeks should really absorb the famous dictum by the Athenian orator Isocrates (438-336 BC), which, in its entirety, runs as follows:

"Our city has made the name of Greeks signify not the origin but the intellect so that Greeks are called those who partake in our culture rather than those who are of the same extraction as us."

This was, and is, a tall order. The national identity (the Greeks call it "national consciousness") of a people, like the muscular physique of an athlete, is defined through constant effort and training. It is forged rather than given. The strong "tribal" element in it reflects its extended family origins. Without getting down to the minutiae of "ethnogenesis" - stock in trade of sociologists and anthropologists - one can safely say that as nations acquire charters defining rights and duties, the notion of belonging to a given nation changes. How to combine the virtues of assimilation with those of cultural diversity then becomes a challenge.

Native Greeks are often annoyed when their Greek-American relatives on visit in their mother country behave, think and act like Americans. They call them *brooklides* (Brooklyn-dwellers), which is not exactly a term of endearment.

The day a Hellenised Albanian (a recent one, not one of the Arvanites of 500 years ago who are as Greek as they come) will visit Tirana and behave like a Greek-American in Athens, Greeks will have embarked for good on defining themselves the Isocratic way, by assimilating the *xenoi* who have come to Greece in recent years.

The Greeks have a word for it: Xenophobia

Those opposing migrant labour should be frank and admit that they have no arguments, only naked unashamed prejudice. What they could say in mitigation would be that they are but the victims of Greek schooling that teaches them Greeks are the salt of the earth and that all non-Greeks are barbarians who should be kept at bay

HERE is a story that this columnist heard a year ago from the horse's mouth. Pity he cannot name the horse.

Police stations in Attica found themselves dealing with an inordinate amount of complaint calls about illegal immigrants... on Friday afternoons. Intrigued, some officers investigated the matter. What they found astounded them. The people calling were none other than employers wanting to deprive their illegal immigrant workforce of their paltry weekly wages by having them deported before they got paid! The bosses' civic conscience lay quiescent for four days, but come Friday they were suddenly overwhelmed by a sense of duty towards their country to help rid it of interlopers threatening its much-vaunted ethnic and religious homogeneity. Patriotism in Greece is often, alas, the first and not the last (pace Boswell) refuge of the scoundrel.

Now the truth is that employers all over the world simply love illegal immigrants, since these do not complain when paid peanuts, cost nothing in social security contributions and do as they are told, living in constant fear of deportation. In Greece, there is so much hostility against the Other that unscrupulous bosses can both have their cake and eat it. They can - illegally - exploit immigrants and, at the same time, pose as defenders of the law and the "purity of Greece". They thus make a profit banking on xenophobia.

The opinion polls are depressing. One funded by the EU and carried out in 2003 in Greece between January 20 and March 15 by the National Centre for Social Research found that 82.7 percent of Greeks believe no foreigners, or very few, of different race should be allowed to live in the country. The relevant percentage in the Netherlands was then 41.0 percent. Should society be made up of different religions? No, say 60.2 percent of Greeks and only 19.5 percent of Dutch.

Greek respondents gave the usual "reasons" to justify their answers: "Immigrants are a drain on the economy" is one of them. Utter rubbish. The exact opposite is true. As the diligent Kathy Tzilivakis showed in an excellent report on immigration in the *Athens News* on 19 September 2003, the Greek economy would collapse if the 9.4 percent of the workforce in Greece composed of immigrants were to leave. Native Greeks are after state jobs that pay well and make minimal demands on them. Meanwhile, poorly paid immigrants pick, cut, wash and pack vegetables all over Greece under the scorching sun, gladly doing the jobs that native Greeks consider beneath them.

When the mayor of Hydra - reports Tzilivakis - decided to hire rubbish collectors in the early '90s, not a single native responded to the job ad. As of a year ago, the mayor revealed, there were 16 Albanian immigrants employed who are indispensable and fully integrated in the local community. So are hundreds of thousands who work night shifts at petrol stations, serve clients at shops and customers in restaurants, lay bricks, work in hotels and keep the wheels of the economy turning as former labour minister Dimitris Reppas explained often and at length. Their contribution is invaluable and not only because they work more for less. As Professor Rosettos Fakiolas of the Athens National Technical University has found in a study of the socio-economic aspects of immigration in Greece, immigrants - as opposed to natives - display a "high job and geographical mobility as they tend to flock to areas of high casual demand for labour with low job qualifications". Truth be told, immigrants help create jobs by allowing small businesses, which would otherwise have gone under, to survive.

"Everybody knows that the immigrants are welfare-scroungers" is another stock-in-trade piece of utter nonsense. The truth is immigrants help keep the social security system afloat. Being under 45 years of age, able-bodied and healthy, they contribute a whopping 1 billion euros annually to the country's social security funds, while making minimal demands on them. Most of today's immigrants will return anyway to their country of origin long before they qualify for an old-age pension.

Let us face it: immigration is a win-win game. It helps the sender countries, which benefit from the immigrants' remittances; it helps the immigrants earn good money and save; and it helps the receiving country, Greece, in all sorts of ways. Those opposing migrant labour should be frank and admit that they have no arguments, only naked unashamed prejudice. What they could say in mitigation would be that they are but the victims of Greek schooling that teaches them Greeks are the salt of the earth and always have been from times immemorial, and that all non-Greeks are barbarians who should be kept at bay lest they pollute by their presence the purity of the Greek race or challenge the absolute truths of the Greek Orthodox faith.

As if that was not enough, there came along an Albanian schoolkid in 2003 who outperformed all his mates and was still not allowed to carry the Greek flag, as a native would, during a national holiday. Isocrates' dictum that Greeks are those partaking of Greek culture is poor consolation for native Greeks who partake of very little culture anyway. The polls are instructive in this regard. The higher the education level of the respondents, the less their xenophobia. Now, "Analyse This" please...

II) Hostility to strangers gradually being tempered by reason

ANTI-AMERICANISM helps Greek activists keep active. Anti-Catholicism helps the Greek Orthodox Church strengthen its grip on the faithful. Anti-Turkism, however, which used to stand for a "national ideology" in Greece, no longer informs Greek foreign policy in spite of residual rigidities as far as the Aegean question is concerned. Thanks to such reasonable policies, progress is being made on Cyprus while Greece decided no longer to be part of the problem with the Former Yugoslav Republic of Macedonia in the Balkans. In fact, as Greece becomes slowly proficient in the art of compromise, the need for heroes in each generation is significantly reduced. There is, one could say, a welcome course from hero to zero demand both for the practice and the rhetoric of heroics.

The 'uses' of anti-Americanism

The truth is that after September 11, unbeknownst to the demonstrating Greeks, all has gone suddenly very quiet on the Western front of protest

VIRTUALLY everybody knows by now what demonstrators in Athens are against: the Americans, of course. What they are for is less clear and never shouted. In fact, they believe that nothing much should be done against terrorists, who happen to hate America too. However, even political morons must have realised by now that to allow such terrorists to operate with impunity is not an innocuous policy option. Doing nothing while Iraqi "resistance fighters" – as the Greek media insist on calling them – decapitate women hostages in the areas they control, and while Al Qa'ida's suicidal fanatics aspire to gain access to nuclear material is not without cost.

To advocate patience, to think that these people could be stopped if only the US did this, that or the other (there is a wide variety of proposed prescriptions for the American behaviour modification programme), to assume that terrorism can be pacified by a mixture of admonition, empathy and therapy is unconvincing, no matter how often and how stridently war is exorcised by frenzied crowds outside the American Embassy in Athens.

For Osama bin Laden to indoctrinate and train suicide pilots is one thing. For his supporters in Greece to preach to his potential victims to commit suicide by default, i.e. to wait helplessly for the suicidal maniacs to strike, is quite another.

The truth is that after September 11, unbeknownst to the demonstrating Greeks, all has gone suddenly very quiet on the Western front of protest. According to one US activist by the name of Kevin Danaher, "the movement is shifting into educational mode". Another such, named Robert Weisman, is even blunter: "We are all a footnote right now." They have remained so even after the US and UK blunders about the elusive "weapons of mass destruction" have been exposed on prime time TV around the world.

Not so for the motley group of Greek "footnotes" who still think of themselves as foot-soldiers. No "respectful pause" for them, no reassessment of priorities, and no departure from the motto of the lady who heads the Greek Communist Party that "neither mirth nor tears" was the appropriate reaction to the Twin Towers falling down.

This is perhaps inevitable: activists need to keep active. The combination of anti-war and anti-Americanism is a heady mixture as it combines righteous anger and Vietnam nostalgia in equal doses. So, while bin Laden continues to exhort Muslims to join his "holy war", the Athens street-shows will go on. This, in a way, is as it should be. In Greece, an EU member, those who oppose their government and its allies can demonstrate and shout until they are blue in the face. In Afghanistan under the Taliban and in Iraq under Saddam, dissidents acquired this particular face colouring much more speedily when they were unceremoniously hanged without a trial. Anti-Americanism has multiple "uses" not just in Greece but throughout the world. Political uses, in that it helps self-definition. National uses, in that it helps local elites resist modernisation and change. Collective uses, as it cements a variety of protest movements into one. Personal uses, as it enhances cultural snobbery in complex-ridden, low-calibre, publicity-hungry intellectuals. Socio-economic uses, as it can stifle developments that might endanger antiquated value-systems consolidating the power of vested interests. In short, blessed anti-Americanism can be valuable in organising resistance to outside influences and securing the entrenchment of local power structures.

A friend of this columnist wondered in an e-mail message whether some Greeks indulge in anti-Americanism because they are fearful of the American model of the open society. Could it be that they feel threatened by what American imports - if left unchecked - might entail for Greek tradition and identity? These are serious questions. They relate to the dual aspect of Modern Greece ever since she became a nation-state with Byzantium and the West drawing her in different (opposite?) directions. To "analyse this", however, would be another story, as Kipling would say.

Hostility between Christian churches not mandatory

*The original theological dispute is by now well beyond
the attention span of the average Catholic
or Orthodox Christian*

WHAT exactly is it that fuels the hostility of the Orthodox priesthood in Greece and Russia against the Roman Catholics? Why is Vartholomeos, the Ecumenical Patriarch, on such good terms with the Pope, while the Greek Orthodox Church and the Russian one are at daggers drawn with Catholicism? Every now and again there is mention in the press about the dogmatic differences separating Eastern from Western Christendom, but these are rarely spelled out. There are good reasons for this reticence, as it makes very little sense today.

The original theological dispute about whether the Holy Spirit proceeds solely from the Father, as the Orthodox believe, or from both the Father and the Son, as the Roman Catholics say, is by now well beyond the attention span of the average member of either denomination. The only real stumbling block to smoother relations that Archbishop Christodoulos attempted to raise with the Pope, when he met him in Athens on 4 May 2001 – a meeting that went rather well, as the Pope "apologised" profusely for the Fourth Crusade that ransacked Constantinople in 1204 - seems to have been that of the Eastern Rite Catholic (Uniate) Church. The Orthodox consider the Uniates (not exceeding 2,000 in Greece), who follow the Orthodox rites but pledge their allegiance to the Pope, as agents of the Catholic Church trying to recruit good Orthodox souls by deceit. However, the Orthodox should remind themselves from time to time of some uncomfortable facts of their own church's history.

There was a brief period when the official Church of the Eastern Roman Empire, later dubbed Byzantium, was part of the one, unified, catholic (a Greek word meaning "universal") Church mentioned in the Creed. The Union of the Churches that brought together the Eastern and Western wings of Christendom was concluded at the Ferrara-Florence Council in July 1439. The Eastern Rites were preserved, but the Pope was recognised as the head of the unified church, just as happens with the Uniates today who have remained loyal to the agreement establishing the Union of the Churches.

The late Sir Stephen Runciman draws a poignant picture of the last ever Mass of the United Church held in Aghia Sophia the day before Constantinople fell to the Ottomans. He describes how the faithful came out in the streets carrying on their shoulders their icons and relics. He adds that "the throng that followed behind them, Greeks and Italians, Orthodox and Catholic, sang hymns and repeated the Kyrie Eleisson". The emperor Constantine Palaeologos spoke from the heart. He said he was prepared to die and thanked the Italians under Giuliani (usually dismissed as "mercenaries" by the Orthodox historians even though they fought valiantly against the Ottomans and saw their leader Giuliani die in battle) for their heroic fight against the enemy. He then "walked slowly round the chamber, asking each one to forgive him if ever he had caused offence". People were kissing each other goodbye. The ceremony was attended even by those Greeks who had been so infuriated by the Ferrara-Florence accords that they had not set foot in Aghia Sophia for years, and had thus avoided witnessing the Sacred Liturgy defiled, as they believed, by Latins and renegades.

The next day Constantinople fell. The Ottoman rulers made sure thereafter that the Orthodox Church remained bitterly hostile not just to Catholicism but also to all things Western.

Ever since, however, missionaries of monastic orders (Jesuits, Dominicans, Franciscans) have kept alive the concept of the United Church. The Brest-Litovsk Union of 1596 - under which all but two Ukrainian Orthodox bishops submitted to the demand of their Polish Catholic king to accept the primacy of the Pope - signalled the effective advent of the Eastern Rite (Uniate) churches that have spread throughout Eastern Europe and the Middle East. A Polish-born Pope - or any Pope for that matter - could hardly ever agree to abolish the Uniate Church.

Orthodox and Catholics could, however, agree to disagree on this issue and keep their relations brotherly in a Christian spirit. This is the stance of Patriarch Vartholomeos in Istanbul. Would it really be so demeaning for the Greek Orthodox Church to follow his lead for once?

Making history happen...

Unlike Iraq, Turkey is a country that already has foundations on which to build a secular democratic Muslim state, a government of impeccable Islamic credentials willing to try and a neighbour ready to help it achieve its goal

A MONGST the routine courtesies exchanged when Greek ministers meet their Turkish counterparts are pledges to change the history books, often full of hate, and promises not to allow the past to shape the future.

This is a tall order because those who, in both countries, resent and attempt to undermine a Greco-Turkish rapprochement invariably do so in the name of History (with a capital H). The trouble is that history as used in political debate (and frequently in academia too) seldom refers to what happened, or even to what (often biased) historians said had happened, but very often to what present-day demagogues insist happened. This leads, at best, to a policy of staying put. By doing nothing, a politician usually risks nothing, but then, as somebody said, "a ship in harbour is safe but that is not what ships are built for." This stance has already started to change, as on 18 December 2004 all the EU countries, including Greece and the Republic of Cyprus, decided to give Turkey the 3 October 2005 as the starting date for her entry negotiations.

This also requires a drastic change of attitude in the way of looking at Greco-Turkish relations. History, as it is taught in Greece - and probably in Turkey too - sees the relations between the two countries as a zero-sum game. What is good for one side is bad for the other. It also teaches Greeks, although this is rarely mentioned, that ever since the fall of Constantinople in AD1453, whenever the Greeks fought the Turks alone, they were beaten. On the other hand, whenever the Greeks had allies and relied on the help of western European powers in their confrontation with Turkey, they won. Now that the era of armed conflict between European nations is over, Greece has been significantly helped in her problems with Turkey by involving outsiders (especially the EU) in the quest for solutions. Turkey's progress in Europeanisation has shown that the stronger the influence of Brussels on Ankara, the better for everybody concerned. Zero-sum games have thus become, er... history. Both the Simitis government and even more so the present New

Democracy one, as well as the Turkish government headed by Mr Erdogan, seem to have grasped this, thank God and Allah.

Contrary to what it had promised to deliver, the Kemalist system of government in Turkey (secular political parties dominated by a coup-prone army) proved incapable (unable, unwilling or both) to turn Turkey into a country implementing European values. In 2002, Turkish voters, fed up with the stagnant and corrupt status quo, provided a strong majority to an outsider, namely the Justice and Development Party (AKP), with Muslim roots that promised to bring Turkey into the European fold. What conventional wisdom had not foreseen was the fact that Turkey's Islamists, who had been at the receiving end of Kemalist bans and persecutions of all kinds, would embrace the European emphasis on human rights with such passion

As a result, the AKP-led Turkish parliament has so far adopted important reforms. The progress may have been at times patchy, but it is there, even if the Turkish prime minister has had to throw, from time to time, some rhetorical red meat to the Grey Wolves snapping at his heels. Torture is banned, even if some of those still practising it can sometimes get away with it; broadcasts in Kurdish are allowed, even if they are full of official propaganda; the death penalty is eliminated; and the role of the military, which has always dominated the National Security Council, has been curtailed, and this deeply anti-democratic institution that enshrines the armed forces' supervisory role in the country's governance is now almost safely under civilian control.

The "European" Turks hail such measures as being long overdue and good in themselves. The others tolerate them at best, provided they lead Turkey into the EU. "What is the point of changing our methods of governance," they ask, "if after all we are refused entry into this Christian club that is the EU?" Attitudes such as the one adopted by Giscard d' Estaing that "accepting Turkey would be the end of Europe" are only encouraging the die-hards in Turkey. The core of the opposition to Turkey's accession to the EU is the fear (particularly in Germany and France) that Turkish immigrants would flood western Europe if ever the free movement of Turks were allowed.

Such fears are exaggerated. Turkey will not be a net exporter of labour forever. Anyway, starting negotiations with Turkey does not mean that accession is imminent. It took Spain and Portugal eight years from the start of negotiations to their admission. Turkey will probably need double that time to sort out its messy, state-controlled economy.

Even after Turkey becomes a member, the EU decided on 18 December 2004 that it could insist for a reasonable transition period before the free flow of labour is implemented. The real, but suppressed, worry is that Turkey is too large a Muslim country to fit into the EU. Paradoxically, this is exactly what makes its membership so interesting.

The future of Muslim countries is no longer an academic issue. The project to turn Iraq into a model secular democratic Muslim state has proven so far a somewhat elusive aspiration. Turkey, on the other hand, is a Muslim country that already has foundations on which to build, a government of impeccable Islamic credentials willing to try, and a neighbour - Greece - ready to help it achieve this goal. Leaders in both countries wishing to make history - rather than remain prisoners to a biased interpretation of it - can now make things happen. This is marginally more creative than just letting things happen.

Athens, Nicosia in a win-win situation...
if they play their cards right

Could Turkey ever trust a supranational institution enough to accept its decisions on matters of national importance to it? Could it permanently resist the temptation to use the threat of force to have its way?

HELMUT Kohl used to muse in private that Turkey would never be accepted into the EU because it is "too large, too populous, too poor and too Muslim". More recently, Valery Giscard d'Estaing said in public that Turkey "does not belong in Europe".

One cannot help but wonder how politicians form their opinions. There was a time when the Ottoman Empire was dubbed "the sick man of Europe", and nobody objected to this except, perhaps, the Sultan whose diagnosis was different.

Should we perhaps rename the empire posthumously as "the sick man of Asia"? This would be a misnomer because Asia contained then - and now - much more serious cases. Unlike Morocco with which it has been compared, Turkey has long been a member of the Council of Europe. When it became an associate member of the EC in 1964, it was not asked to shrink, rid itself of its excess population, get richer and (Allah forbid) embrace Christianity in order to qualify.

Thirty-five years later, Turkey's European status was further confirmed. In 1999, the European Council in Helsinki decided unanimously that Turkey should be a candidate for membership to the EU "destined to join the Union on the basis of the same criteria as applied to the other candidate states". Nowhere was geography, population size or religion mentioned.

Nonetheless, Turkey's candidacy brought to the fore two important issues. The first concerns what it means to be European. The notion that the EU is only a community of values is obviously wrong. Could for instance Japan, New Zealand, South Africa or Canada apply? A geographical component is, for the time being, a necessary condition unless the EU decides to spread its wings worldwide as did the North Atlantic Treaty Organisation, which has long included countries that cannot see the North Atlantic even with binoculars. So, even a toehold on geographic Europe will do for Turkey, especially as its "toe" contains more people than Greece, Cyprus, Malta and Luxembourg combined.

The second issue has to do with the paramount importance of the 1993 Copenhagen criteria that a candidate must fulfil to qualify for negotiations to start. The summit held in Copenhagen on 12-13 December 2002 gave Turkey a chance - and plenty of time - to achieve "stability of institutions guaranteeing democracy, the rule of law, human rights and respect for as well as protection of minorities". No concessions on value fundamentals were made, and no pressure from the US could ever coerce the European Council to give in on this.

OK, some may say, but is it really possible for Turkey to change so much as to accept the European way of solving problems by argument and reaching solutions by compromise? Could Turkey ever trust a foreign institution enough to accept its decisions on matters of national importance to it? Could it ever resist the temptation to use the threat of force to have its way?

The answer is maybe. Countries and their people change. A Western traveller to Japan in the early 19th century described its inhabitants as fishermen so convinced of the value of their traditions that they would never be able to accept any innovation to improve their fishing methods.

The Turkey that would one day join the EU would be a totally different Turkey than it ever was. Change is already happening there to the consternation and cold fury of the traditionalists. Who will win depends crucially on the external help that the reformists can get. Had President Mohammad Khatami of Iran been able to draw on outside support (he already commands huge popular majorities at home), he would have restricted his own die-hard conservatives to quarters long time ago. It would be a pity if Turkey's "modernisers" were to suffer the same fate.

For Athens and Nicosia, if they continue to play their cards right, a Turkey dependent on the goodwill of the EU and trying to conform to its rules of behaviour is a win-win situation. If reform is achieved and Turkey changes, fine. If it fails, then the EU as a whole will have to deal with it, try and contain Turkey's aggressive elements and help the reformers fight another day. Either way, Athens and Nicosia will never again have to face on their own such a dangerous problem-country as Turkey has been in the past.

Greece needs heroes no longer

Compromise became in Greek a dirty word, almost a synonym for treason. So much so, in fact, that Karamanlis (the elder) got into trouble in the 1970s when striving for a 'compromis' to bring the Aegean dispute to the International Court at The Hague

WHAT dawns on Greeks these days is that their country looks, feels, nay is, normal. This marks a change. Since 1909, Greece had to endure some 22 military coups, three dictatorships, two Balkan wars, the Asia Minor Catastrophe, two world wars, the Nazi occupation, a bloody civil war and the 1974 events that brought the Turkish army into Cyprus. Since then, the Greek volcano has been quiescent, if not altogether dormant.

During its active phase, the volcano spewed up a variety of heroes - and villains. Greeks eventually learned to appreciate two lines from Bertolt Brecht's Galileo: "Andrea: Unhappy the land that has no heroes! - Galileo: No, unhappy the land that needs heroes." During their "heroic" times Greeks got accustomed to the use of violence for political goals, playing deadly zero sum games in which the choice was always between sacrifice and surrender. The first step towards expulsion from the Communist party was to accuse someone of being of "reduced intransigence" (*μειωμένης αδιαλλαξίας*). Activists were expected to give their heart to, and spill their blood for, the Cause. Demands on their brains were minimal. This columnist remembers a leading member of EDA (the broad left including the communists, active in the '50s and '60s) complaining that the clandestine Communist party whose leadership was in Romania was fast becoming the party of "heroic jerks" (*κόμμα των πρωϊκών κοπάνων*). In the other camp, the "national-minded" (*εθνικόφρων*) right was always suspicious of intellectuals, considering them fellow-travellers, unless they could prove otherwise.

Compromise became in Greek a dirty word, almost a synonym for treason. So much so, in fact, that Karamanlis (the elder) got into trouble in the 1970s when striving for a compromis to bring the Aegean dispute to the International Court at The Hague. It took some time for his critics to realise that this French legal term was simply close, etymologically, to the original sense of the word meaning "double promise", in this case an agreement by both parties to bring the dispute to the court and abide by its decision.

So when did Greece (if not yet the Greeks) abandon the "heroic" attitude of "all or nothing - now or never"? Some say that the new "managerial age" of pursuing national interests (and not "national-mindedness") through patient diplomacy, merging them into those of a larger community such as the EU and banking on the might of argument rather than on the argument of (usually non-existent) might, started in 1981 when Greece became a member of the EC as it then was. However, Greece's first steps in Europe were difficult. Andreas Papandreou, displaying his own nationalistic brand of populism and pursuing a policy of "one foot in, one foot out" as the *Financial Times* described it, lost no time in having Greece branded as the "reluctant partner", the "problem case" or the "black sheep" of the Community during the 1980s. To quote George Pagoulatos - an assistant professor at the Athens University of Economics and Business - from a very interesting article published in Jacques Delors' Notre Europe: "Some branded Greece as 'the country of footnotes' for its tendency to dissociate itself from common Council communiques... Greece was considered as the EU's weakest link. Its marginalisation inside the EU was taken for granted, its failure to meet the EMU objectives was predicted as certain and several pundits were even playing with the idea of Greece becoming the first member ever to be ejected from the EU."

In the early '90s, the verbal onslaught against a small neighbouring country that dared use the word "Macedonia" in its name culminated in the idiotic embargo against it by none other than Papandreou (re-elected in 1993), marking Greece's severe relapse in its "heroic" bungling of relations with a neighbouring country. That is why some prefer to date the end of the "heroic age" and the start of the new "managerial era" to 1995, when relations with the Former Yugoslav Republic of Macedonia were normalised. Others place it in December 1999 when Greece agreed at the Helsinki summit to invite Turkey to become an EU candidate. The 2002 Copenhagen summit consolidated Greece in her new role. So Greeks must now make up their minds whether to treat their heroes as icons they should revere or models they should follow.

III) Greek levellers hate only the wealth of others

Greeks have been taught by left wing intellectuals and politicians to hate "elites" unless they belong to one and to resent wealth creation by others, even if this is achieved by entirely legitimate means. Many of them, given a choice, will opt for job security rather than profit making that involves taking risks. They dislike the free market and abhor redundancy. They are not averse making life unbearable to foreign investors; they love it when an incompetent minister starts browbeating businessmen in public and never stop claiming subsidies and state protection. As long as such attitudes prevail, the extraordinary success of the Irish model of development via the market will remain comfortably alien to Greece's rulers and ruled alike.

Is wealth creation a crime?

The aversion of the party's voters to PASOK officials lining their own pockets even led them to resent when these tried to make money by legitimate means

IN A pre-war French film by Marcel Pagnol, Raimu - a gifted actor - tells his well-dressed interlocutor: "The difference between us socialists and your lot is that while you think of yourselves as owners of your personal fortune, we consider ourselves as the trustees of ours."

In Greece, such a distinction would be too subtle to explain to the masses. Therefore, ever since Andreas Papandreou launched his PASOK (Panhellenic Socialist Movement - no longer any of the above), Greek socialists have entertained a love-hate relationship with money. They have all been vituperating against it in public but far too many of them embraced it with passion in private.

To begin with, Andreas used an astute approach to endear himself to millions of Greeks. He poised himself as the champion of the "unprivileged". This term sounded vaguely familiar to assorted leftists fed on a literature of class war but also pleased all those, irrespective of means, status and profession, who covet somebody else's success in life.

The contradiction inherent in this slogan bothered nobody. Was this a policy to abolish privilege (thus making everybody equally poor as in the Soviet Union) or was it a pledge to make everybody privileged, reminiscent of the promise by that statistically challenged politician who had promised to raise everybody's income above average? No matter.

There was, however, never much clarity as to whether the members of PASOK, its deputies, its tens of thousands of appointees in local government, public corporations and banks ever came under the rubric of "unprivileged" and in need of sustenance. The fact is that when some of them started gorging themselves at the taxpayer's expense, Andreas drew the line. He said unofficially and with a smile that PASOK officials should not appropriate more than 500 million Drs for their personal needs.

While there was still money (increasingly borrowed) sloshing around in the 1980s, few seemed to mind and continued with these practices until such time as the increased deficits, high borrowing, inflation and the threat of collapse brought about unavoidably painful austerity measures. As a result, the public's tolerance of PASOK officials' personal enrichment started to plunge dramatically. Simitis, a man of great personal integrity, tried his best – which eventually proved not good enough – to restrain his more lax comrades from shoddy practices at the expense of the taxpayers. He failed because the rot had gone too deep. The party's voters felt let down. Their aversion to PASOK officials lining their own pockets even led them to resent when these tried to make money by legitimate means. Victims of this revolt of the unprivileged were Manikas and Neonakis in June 2003, who were unceremoniously dumped from their governmental posts when a populist daily revealed the sums they had speculated on the Athens Stock Exchange four years before. There was no impropriety involved, no insider dealing and no abuse of their official position. Ironically, they did not even make money but lost substantial amounts, together with millions of other Greeks during the boom and bust of the Athens Stock Exchange.

At that point, not all Greeks were losers, of course. For instance, Dimitris Koufodinas, star defendant at the November 17 murderers' trial, made then 14 million Drs on the stock exchange, as was revealed in court, at about the time the two PASOK officials were sacrificed. But then, he, of all people, could well be expected to make a killing.

To improve PASOK's image in view of the elections that were to follow, Simitis decided to clear the decks. He thus announced that the system checking the origins of a person's assets, which now applies to MPs, would be extended to many thousands more and start restrictively as of 1998, before the boom. This system known by the misnomer *pothen esches* (whence your possessions) has rarely, if ever, obliged anyone to account for the provenance of their worldly goods. It simply requires that these be recorded. Even this has proved meaningless, as files pile up with no one assigned even to glance at them, let alone check them out. To be fair, however, to the two aides who had been ousted, they never concealed anything. So the extension of *pothen esches* achieved nothing more than appointing teams of incompetent civil servants to   rummage helplessly through heaps of often illegible "annual declarations".

There is worse. Without going so far as to say that "property is theft", as good old Pierre-Joseph Proudhon wrote in 1844, the distinction between profiteering (*aischrokerdeia*) and profit-making became distinctly blurred under PASOK's rule. Championed by Kimon Koulouris - a PASOK reject who was kept out of harm's way for years and was brought back in 2003 at the development ministry to hunt for "profiteers" - market regulation started raising its ugly head. To keep Brussels at bay, this started as "voluntary" but with Koulouris on the loose, Greeks started to get really frightened, having lived through many an unenforceable price regulation attempt that bred corruption and the emergence of a black market.

Somebody ought to explain to the Greeks that legitimate wealth creation is good; that it is a condition for Greece to grow, prosper and achieve the much longed for convergence with its EU partners. Is anybody listening at the New Democracy Party headquarters now that their party is in power, or are they all toiling hard to get appointed to public sector jobs while Karamanlis - to his credit - tries to keep them at bay?

In Greece, Sisyphus enjoys security of tenure

European leaders should realise, at long last, that the lag in their economies was due to a combination of rigidities in labour and product markets, high labour costs imposed by governments, low productivity and high taxes to finance the state's interference in the economy

THE EUROBAROMETER reports of recent years keep confirming that Greeks worry about unemployment. So they should, with 9.5 percent of them being out of work. So did the PASOK government, and so do their heirs in New Democracy.

Years ago, when Professor Spraos - who had been asked by then prime minister Costas Simitis to take a long, hard look at Greece's socio-economic problems - came up with some ideas of how to combat unemployment, he was greeted by a section of the press and trade unionists with the same mixture of derision, hostility and fear that often stands for "dialogue" in Greece.

Instead of recommending mass appointments in the public sector, the good professor dared suggest that the Greek jobless be helped to become "employable". They should be trained, he proposed, in the new technologies to acquire the proper marketable skills that would help them find jobs in the private sector.

In Lisbon, on 24 March 2000, the European leaders, with only Lionel Jospin dragging his socialist feet, agreed to do just that. UK Prime Minister Tony Blair said the summit marked a "sea change in EU economic thinking". Simitis said that jobs could only be created by economic growth and praised the US model that brought unemployment down to a derisory 4 percent (in the EU it was then close to 10 percent).

The Lisbon summit did indeed bury unceremoniously the venerable remains of the Keynesian orthodoxy, with its emphasis on cash injections to stimulate demand and on creating jobs artificially, if necessary, whether they had a purpose or not (like opening holes in the ground and then closing them up again, a variant of Sisyphus' job description).

In Greece, the preferred option was to appoint tens of thousands - preferably party hacks - to loss-making public corporations where they had little to do except party or trade union chores. There was never a justification for this. Even the ancient Greeks did not consider the myth of Sisyphus as a policy option but as a warning.

In Lisbon, Europe's leaders, including a Simitis who waxed lyrical on the subject, declared a "new strategic goal". The EU, they decided, should "become the most competitive and dynamic knowledge-based economy in the world", alluding to the need to catch up with the US.

They had some serious catching up to do but didn't. The American "goldilocks economy" based on fast productivity growth and low inflation had been partly the result of a massive investment boom. Between 1990 and 1999, business investment in the US almost doubled in real terms; in the EU, it rose by only 16 percent. The most important change needed in Europe was a change of mind. European leaders should realise at long last that the lag in their economies was due to a combination of rigidities in labour and product markets, high labour costs imposed by governments, low productivity and high taxes to finance the state's interference in the economy.

So what happened after Lisbon? Not much. Job creation worldwide continued to be at its best in economies where labour mobility was high and "job protection" minimal. In the US, which continues to lead the world in this field, redundant workers are paid about four days' wages for each year that they have been with a company. Compare this to Germany where courts can award sacked employees up to 18 months' pay (for those over 55 with 20 years service).

In Greece, the departing handshake is so "golden" that firms needing to downsize can only afford to sack their most recent recruits even if those happen to be the most productive. Unemployment benefits in the US are low, so there are four times more job applications from people on the dole than in Britain, where benefits are generous. An OECD report published in April 2002 showed that economies with low-cost redundancy provisions (Australia, US, Canada and Ireland, to mention the top four) created far more new jobs than those which make layoffs time-consuming and expensive.

Lisbon, then, resulted in a lot of hot air. The American workforce remains "employable" and increases its productivity year in, year out while the number of jobless stays low and the prosperity of those in work high. If shorter hours, higher guaranteed minimum wage, longer holidays and barriers to dismissal were a cure for unemployment, Europe should enjoy the world's lowest rate. Instead, it has the highest among developed nations, and Greece among the highest in the EU.

Professor Spraos was right. Greece's unemployed had better absorb his message and strive to become "employable". There is no salvation in the quack medicines offered by the promoters of Sisyphus, this "proletarian of the gods, powerless and rebellious" condemned to know "the whole extent of his wretched condition", as Albert Camus put it in his prophetic "Le Mythe de Sisyphe", written in 1942.

'Much pain and no gain' is no way to attract investors

If Greece is 47th among 50 OECD nations in competitiveness and last in the EU in foreign direct investment, that is because she wants to be

HOW to make Greece more competitive" was the question on the minds of the participants at a one-day conference held in May 2002 at the Inter-Continental Hotel in Athens. It was organised by the active, non-political Association of Chief Executive Officers (ACEO), founded in 1986 - the only body that represents top managers of businesses established in Greece.

Young executives came from Procter and Gamble, Unilever, Microsoft and other such multinationals and nationals keen for answers. They proved to be a questioning bunch, part of a new breed of Greeks, workaholics but also relaxed, self-assured but inquisitive, serious in purpose but jocular in attitude, viewing with amused condescension the occasional outbreaks of anti-capitalist hype in Greece and with barely controlled irritation the thousand and one obstacles put in their way by the country's main commodity: red tape.

Their English, incidentally, ranged from excellent to perfect. Their Greenglish could be funny. One thus heard some of them saying that the no-nonsense speech by one of the guest speakers, Lester Thurrow (MIT professor of management and economics) was "entyposiastic" (impressive), an adjective formed on the pattern of "enthusiastic" from the Greek word *entyposi* (impression).

"You must realise," the American professor told his audience, "that 10 million people do not make a significant market. To draw inflows you have to offer something special... Ireland has very low taxes, Singapore has the least amount of bureaucracy in the world (you can set up a company there in one morning), Taiwan's manufacturing efficiency is unparalleled, Israel boasts some of the best brains in the world. What has Greece to offer apart from the Parthenon which is spectacular?"

The round-table discussion that followed brought up the usual litany of complaints: bureaucracy, corruption, a baffling tax system... In a private conversation one of the participants suggested a system to make tax forms simpler. Rumour has it, he said, that in Britain a tax form is first written by the cleverest civil servant in the ministry and then read by the most "intellectually challenged" of them all. If the latter failed to understand it, the form should be returned to the former as often as necessary for further simplification.

This might create difficulties in Greece because who would ever admit to qualify as a "reader"? Perhaps, somebody suggested, the matter could be referred to a party organisation where idiots are never in short supply.

The wise Hans Dietrich Genscher, former German foreign minister, also a guest speaker, was categorical. "What is needed," he said, "to make Greece competitive, is political will."

He can say that again. If Greece is 47th among 50 OECD nations in competitiveness and last in the EU in foreign direct investment, that is because she wants to be.

"We will not become like Ireland," former PM Costas Simitis pledged shortly before the conference. Indeed. Who in his right mind wants to upset local traditions and turn the country upside down just to raise the annual per capita income of its citizens from $3,000 in 1984 to $17,000 in 2002 as Ireland did? Better to kick out foreign companies as happened to Italian Pirelli from Patra and Canadian TVX from northern Greece. This is called "being responsive to local feeling".

Two days before the ACEO conference, Nikos Christodoulakis, then Greece's economy and finance minister, who personally would have very much wanted to put Greece on Ireland's path if only his party had let him, addressed the Federation of Greek Industries (SEB) with his tongue firmly in cheek. To quote from the report in the *Athens News* (31 May 2002, by Harry Papachristou) "'Privatisations? Yes, but with the handbrake pulled up...Tax reform? Expect simpler rules but no lower rates. Market liberalisation? Fine in principle but not an option before the government is convinced it leads to lower prices and better services. Reforms must come in small doses in order to draw public support,' Christodoulakis cautioned."

During the Networking Cocktail that followed the round-table discussion, the young executives flocked around the guest speakers as if to draw strength from them. They needed it for the years ahead...

How Greece kicks foreign investors in the teeth

The multiplicity of laws and regulations, the bureaucracy and the lack of structural reforms in Greece scare potential investors away

ON 17 DECEMBER 2002, the then prime minister Costas Simitis promised that Greece, during its impending stint at the EU presidency, would strive to make the EU "the most competitive market in the world" as the EU summit in Lisbon had decided in 2001.

Here, then, is a true story. Sometime in October 2002 a foreign firm (from Cyprus) decided to invest in Greece. They hired the services of a man, known to this columnist, called George, a Greek expert who happens to sit on the boards of many Greek "societes anonymes". A limited liability partnership was set up, and the venture was launched.

Well, not quite. For the statute of the partnership to be ratified by the court, a "tax for raising capital" had first to be paid, together with the relevant fee to the Welfare Fund of Athenian Lawyers. So far, so bizarre. However, the Greek partner was also told by a bored employee of the Social Security Fund (IKA) that he had to provide documents proving that neither he nor any of the "societes anonymes" he was on the board of, owed any money to IKA. This meant George had to visit in person all the relevant IKA branches one by one.

There was consternation in George's office with the female staff close to tears and the male employees exploding into unprintable expletives. The story has a happy ending though. Such certificates were not needed, after all, for the "societes anonymes". The IKA employee who had asked for them had been recently appointed to his post and had not as yet "fully mastered his brief", according to his apologetic superior.

On 20 October 2003, Odysseas Kyriakopoulos, chairman of the Federation of Greek Industries (SEB), speaking in front of the then national economy minister Nikos Christodoulakis to a gathering of businessmen, denounced once again the multiplicity of laws and regulations, the bureaucracy and the lack of structural reforms in Greece that scare potential investors away.

Had he been less diplomatic, he could have said that the policy of encouraging (!) foreign investment has been entrusted to a bungling

Greek bureaucracy staffed by a mixture of the ignorant, the corrupt, the bored and the devious, endlessly fighting their little turf wars until such time as they all become engulfed in a sea of paperwork. Here are two of their "successes".

When the UK property group, Loyalward, agreed in 1991 with the abbot of the Toplou Monastery in Crete to lease from them for 80 years 6,500 acres of beaches and barren land at Cavo Sidero, little did they know what was in store for them. The project would ultimately include five hotels, 350 villas, 450 apartments, five themed villages, a marina and a sports stadium. This never got off the ground because the state, invoking various forestry laws, claimed ownership of the land even though the monastery had controlled it for hundreds of years through a charitable foundation.

It took eight years of legal battle ending in a decision in 1999 by the Supreme Court to recognise the monastery as the legitimate owner of the land. Speaking to reporters, chairman of Loyalward Christopher Egleton was, in spite of everything, fairly upbeat.

Other investors were less so. Take, for instance, Greenwich Resources, another British firm that won perfectly lawfully the concession to prospect for gold in the (extremely poor) Rodopi region in northern Greece. The firm was astounded to see the environmental impact study being rejected unceremoniously in November 2003 by the local "prefectural council". What was even more galling than the rejection as such was the reason given. As the prefect proudly announced, they had rejected the study not on environmental grounds but on the basis of a "political rationale". They simply did not want foreigners looking for gold in their own backyard.

The Lisbon summit decided, as Simitis cannot have forgotten, to adopt a series of performance indices concerning the inflows of foreign direct investment, public administration, infrastructure, research and technology and liberalisation of markets in every member state. Well, Greece comes last on all of them. And that is not all. On 2 November 2004, the New Democracy Development Minister Mr Sioufas, in a public speech noted that according to a recent UNCTAD report, Greece ranks 137th in the amount of foreign direct investment that it attracts and pointed out that if only the country made good use of its comparative advantages, she could easily climb to the 37th place.

There are hopes that things may improve. To quote Prime Minister Karamanlis in his speech at the Thessaloniki International Trade Fair in

September 2004: "Our aim is to release the creative forces of society," he said, declaring the year 2005 "the year of competitiveness". This will be achieved, he pointed out, by a series of reforms such as a new tax law to encourage investment that will introduce new forms of objective, transparent tax inspections. There will also be a new development law in favour of small and medium sized businesses. Greece's Premier also pledged to abolish the red tape that operates as the main disincentive for investing in Greece and promised to reduce drastically the time needed for starting a business in Greece. According to a World Bank report issued on 9 September 2004, setting up a business in Greece takes 38 days and 15 different procedures, when in Australia, Canada, Denmark and the US only five days are required.

Some forty days before the Premier's address in Thessaloniki, Finance Minister Mr Alogoskoufis, in an interview published in the newspaper *Kathimerini* on 1 August 2004, said that the government's vision was to turn Greece into "the Ireland of the South" attracting foreign investment and becoming the Florida of Europe. His listeners remembered Simitis saying in Parliament when pressed on the subject: "Well, we don't want to end up like Ireland, do we?"

Fresh look at pensions

Wherever in the world social security was privatised, Greece's Liberals pointed out, 'contributions fell, benefits rose and fiscal discipline was respected'

FOR some time in the late nineties and early noughties, the unions in Greece had been clamouring for a "dialogue without preconditions" on social security. As soon as the PASOK government caved in, they dictated their own preconditions: tripartite financing of the system (workers, employers and the state) and lots of fresh money that the government will have to find and pour into it. The then prime minister Mr Simitis gave way.

So what could one expect from such a dialogue on inessentials? Perhaps a few improvements here and there; measures against fraud; the creation of a committee to study the computerisation of records; make immigrants pay their dues; and so on and so boring. The sacred cow of the "pay as you go" system which makes those presently in employment support those who are too old to do so continues no matter how the ratio has worsened. Greek trade unions have so far been adamant: Contributions will not increase, neither will the compulsory retirement age nor will pensions be reduced. As a result the faltering pay-as-you-go system was patched up by PASOK to last a few more years, if that. There are, however, alternatives.

The liberals of Stephanos Manos spelled them out clearly in their newsletter as early as March-April 2001. Every working person, they said, should during his/her working life create through his/her own and his/her employer's contributions a social security capital that will ensure a decent pension. Those who failed to achieve this should be assisted by the state. Contributions would be obligatory but the worker would be free to choose between firms freely competing for his/her custom. Wherever in the world the social security system was privatised, Greece's Liberals pointed out, "contributions fell, benefits rose and fiscal discipline was respected."

At the time, not even New Democracy – the then liberals' partners in opposition - were convinced. As for the rest of the MPs, from PASOK leftwards, their daily-intoned mantras against any intrusion of the private sector into the field of social security continued to be part of the ritual that still passes for public debate on the issue.

It does not have to be this way. For one thing, the profit motive of those who would undertake to manage peoples' money to ensure these would end up with a decent pension is not mandatory. Like some prestigious European universities, pension funds can be independent and provide benefits for their clients only. The important thing is that their management be removed from the hands of incompetent government appointees serving the interests of politicians who rarely think beyond the next election.

Simitis did not have to take his cue from Manos. He could have taken a long careful look at what his fellow social-democrat Gerhard Schroeder had, at that time, been doing in Germany. Despite opposition from various quarters, the chancellor had introduced in May 2001 the most radical reform of social security in Germany for nearly half a century. He had to. Low birth rates and longer life expectancy (does this sound familiar?) had taken their toll in Germany. The number of those at work supporting those who had retired was due to fall in a few years from two working persons per pensioner to one. This was a sure way to the collapse of the system.

So what did Schroeder do? He devised a privately-funded but also state-supported and state-regulated pension scheme. Workers were made to contribute up to 4 percent of their earnings to build their own social security capital and were encouraged to do so with generous tax incentives. In the long run, this parallel system has been calculated to supply as much as 40 percent of overall pension income for Germans with 60 percent still coming through the state, compared with 85 percent today. It was a middle-of-the-way solution between state pensions and totally privatised ones. But even this proved beyond PASOK's powers of adaptation to the modern world. So what Simitis did was to continue the old system with some minor modifications and leave the next government to pull the chestnuts out of the fire.

This has not happened so far. The New Democracy government refuses to comment, mention or even consider the issue of pension funds in Greece. Karamanlis feels insecure about this because he knows that the dinosaurs in his own party would hunt him down mercilessly if he so much as touched on peoples' pensions. Perhaps he waits for the issue to sink in but most probably he holds his horses expecting Brussels to take the necessary but unpopular decisions for all the EU members and thus dictate to Greece what to do. This, he hopes, would take him off the hook and allow him to eschew the (in)famous "political cost" of implementing a liberal, privatised pension scheme.

In the meantime PASOK strategists are putting pressure on their leader, George Papandreou to raise the pensions issue as a stick to hit the government with. Once again one has to hand it to them: They may have lacked guts when in government but they certainly do not lack cheek in opposition!

IV) How the Greek 'nanny state' smothers university education

IN Greece, where "progress" has long been associated with the "nanny state", the state monopoly of wisdom and moral rectitude does not restrict itself to the welfare services and the economy. It extends to the university education of the Greeks. The trouble is that Greek academic teachers strike often, are very relaxed about the hours they teach, and are generally keen to take it easy, as they have no competition and are free of any kind of supervision from any outside body. However, all hope is not lost as both major political parties now agree that non-state universities should be allowed to operate, that lowering the standards of tertiary education in Greece does not pay at a time when the "knowledge revolution" is in full swing and that today's students have to learn not by rote but by looking for the embedded truth in what happens in the world.

Dumbing down - no policy for higher education

Let us agree that it is utopian to attempt to introduce student fees in Greece now. It would not be utopian, though, to allow private universities to operate in Greece alongside the highly regulated, state-run, rigid, costly, inefficient and striking Greek academia

GREEK politicians like to strike a balance, Greek mass media like to strike an attitude and Greek university teachers just like to strike. In 2002 the June examinations were cancelled, as the teachers' union decided should happen. True, their salaries have never been overgenerous, but then the state has accorded them the privilege of working very few hours, as they allegedly need to prepare lectures, pursue their research activities... and organise strikes marginally more efficiently than they organise their work. Most of them prefer to have a good time off campus or work on profitable EU programmes. Nonetheless, they always want more money and benefits. Whenever they complain about the state of Greek higher education, one can be sure their next sentence will be to ask the Greek state to pay them more to deliver it.

The dispute has nothing to do with the real problems of Greece's universities, which, thanks to the collusion of all parties involved, continue to ensure that the standard of the services they offer continues to remain reassuringly low.

In this blessed country university education is not "free" as advertised; only hypocrisy and humbug are. It costs hundreds of millions to the taxpayer. It is a blatant transfer of funds from the have-nots, who overwhelmingly fail to make use of it, to the haves, who could handsomely pay for it.

The system is also inefficient. Not having to pay for goods makes one supremely contemptuous of them. So, Greek students tend to avoid being educated as much as they can. The caring Greek state also provides free books, or rather one free book per course, usually written by the professor. There are no reading lists, because the average Greek professor views his book much like the prophet Mohammed viewed the Quran, as containing all there is to know so that everything not to be found in it is either redundant or false.

In the Greek system there is no limit to the number of times a student can fail. The parents are comfortable with this situation because their offspring can fool around for years on end and still obtain a degree sometime. In a situation where there is no pressure (financial or other) to succeed, there is also no shame in failing. Even so, there are bright spots in this desolate landscape, where some students who wish to learn and some teachers who wish to teach do meet with exceptional (also in the sense of aberrant) results.

Now contrast this with what happens in the US where a friend of this columnist - Professor Thanos Veremis of Athens University - had been the holder throughout 2002 of the Constantine Karamanlis chair of Greek and Balkan Studies at the prestigious Fletcher School of Law and Diplomacy in Boston. What he had to say was astonishing.

Here was a body of students keen to obtain good value for money in their chosen field. Having indebted themselves in order to pursue their university studies, these youngsters were as keen as any consumer to elicit as much as possible from the institution. The university gave them the opportunity to evaluate regularly their professors on all the aspects of their work: coursework, responsiveness to students' queries, their whole professorial performance. Teaching such students, said Veremis, a Greek university teacher since 1977, was really an experience. Interestingly, he got consistently high marks from his students and proved to be very popular with them.

This is not "education for the rich". The gifted poor benefit from generous scholarships in the US private fee-paying universities. This is not education following slavishly the dictates of the market as viewed by intellectual snobs. There is in the US, as elsewhere, a market for goods, computers and cars, but there is also a market for ideas, art and languages - even dead ones. There are in the US eager youngsters who want to become familiar with philosophy, literature, history, and even Balkan politics as the Veremis case showed.

Enough of this comparison. Let us agree that it is utopian to attempt to introduce student fees in Greece now even by a government that has no hang ups with the market and no fixation with state delivered services. It would not be utopian, though, to allow private universities (domestic or foreign) to operate in Greece alongside the highly regulated, state-run, rigid, costly, inefficient and striking Greek academia. Now that both the government of New Democracy and PASOK under the leadership of George Papandreou have agreed in principle to recognise the existence of "non state" universities in Greece, and most crucially on the need to evaluate the services that all Greek Universities offer, one may expect things to change. What a difference it would make to abolish the state monopoly in providing tertiary education to young Greeks, abolish the scandal of the free, single book and the shameful status of the "eternal student"! There might even come a time when the Greek ministry of education would not be under pressure to introduce, pursue and implement the dumbing down policies that students, their families and assorted leftists have so far been imposing on governments of every hue.

All hope is not yet lost for Greece's academia

There are those who hope that the Greek system can be reformed from within. They are mistaken

HERE is a quote from a former "Analyse This" column, dealing with the tendency of Greek university teachers to strike every now and again for higher pay, all in the name of improving Greece's universities of course: "Let us agree it would not be utopian to allow private universities (domestic or foreign) to operate in Greece alongside the highly regulated, state-run, rigid, costly, inefficient - and striking - Greek academia". While things seem to be moving that way in Greece, in a neighbouring country they have already done so with excellent results.

Utopia, as it happens, is not too far away, as Professor Thanos Veremis of Athens University and friend of this columnist found when he visited the capital of neighbouring Turkey in the fall of 2003. There, in a suburb of Ankara, is Bilkent University, modelled on the best US universities. The campus is large and tree-lined, the premises spotless, the professors dedicated to their full-time teaching and research duties, the students hard working and the libraries well-stocked. Prof Veremis was particularly impressed by the fact that each library place was supplied with a set of earphones, thus allowing students to listen to music while reading. In this non-profit making, privately-run Turkish university the lectures are in English, the students pay fees, except for the bright but poor who benefit from generous scholarship schemes. Bilkent University is a success story.

Meanwhile, anecdotal but reliable evidence reaching this columnist from Greek universities plunges one into serious depression. There is the case of the student who was failed seven (yes, seven) times and can keep trying indefinitely. At least the professor who keeps failing him shows some concern about letting graduates such as him loose on an unsuspecting public. Many of his colleagues are much more relaxed about student performance and much more interested in making money in outside jobs, thus letting their assistants do the teaching. One of those sent recently to the lecture room two such assistants - strongly reminiscent of the hilariously incompetent pair described by Kafka in his "Castle" - to teach on his behalf. The first one was so terrorised that he could hardly speak. The second was a loquacious fool, full of himself, who interrupted and corrected his rhetorically challenged colleague so often that the students started making fun of both. The selfsame professor cut his lecture short one day because - as he told the students with some pride in his tremulous voice - he had "an appointment with the minister".

Another time, an evening lecture was cancelled because of a faulty bulb that left the students in the dark...literally this time. No wonder Greek families (some 70,000 thousand of them, last count) bleed themselves white to send their offspring to study abroad. According to the OECD, in 2002 Greece was the country with the most students abroad per million of population, i.e. 5,257, followed by Malaysia with 1,777. Greeks studying in British universities number 25,674 and come first, forming 10 percent of the foreign student population in the UK. In second place are the Chinese with 17,682 students.

There are those who hope that the Greek system can be reformed from within. They are mistaken. Most Greek academics love it because, even if state funded, it allows them total license to look after themselves without any interference from any supervising authority. Students grumble but they too are happy with a system that makes minimal demands upon their time and effort. The fact that they do not learn much does not give many of them sleepless nights because they only want a degree as a passport to a good job in the public sector of the Greek economy. Those eager to get an education rather than just a degree go abroad at some stage. Politicians too are not overwhelmingly distressed by the low standards of many a Greek University as they are glad to control appointments and to spread universities – even just university departments – thin on the ground all over the country, especially in their constituencies. The government of New Democracy that came to power on 7 March 2004 differs at least in its intentions. When push comes to shove, how it will deal with the Greek academic establishment that will never willingly accept to be evaluated by any outsider, remains to be seen.

The picture is not all bleak. Mr Hatzidakis, one of the younger and most enterprising New Democracy's MEPs, rattled in 2003 the Greek academic establishment by securing on November 28 a vote in the Legal Affairs and Internal Market Committee of the European Parliament in favour of the recognition of degrees issued by any institution under franchise or affiliated with a recognised EU university. Such establishments called "liberal studies centres" are allowed to operate in Greece but are supervised by the ministry of trade (not education) and the degrees they issue are not "recognised" by the state. This means that if their graduates apply for a state job they will be treated only as school-leavers.

The Greek constitution specifies that only the state can issue university degrees in Greece. The European Court in Luxembourg begs to differ. In its decision of 13 November 2003 on the case of Valentina Neri (an Italian student that had recourse to the court), it condemned Italy for not recognising degrees issued by local affiliates of recognised universities and clarified that this be considered a precedent for all such cases. Meanwhile in Greece, the Council of State refuses to acknowledge the primacy of European legislation in this instance, and the "progressive" intelligentsia are up in arms to avert any potential challenge to the state's monopoly on university education. What exactly, one wonders, is the Greek academic establishment afraid of? After all, private universities, if allowed, will operate at a disadvantage, as they have to charge for a service that the state provides free.

No matter. Things may change as Greeks begin to realise that fee-paying students in the US - and in Bilkent University for that matter - would never tolerate missing a lecture because of a burned bulb.

Lowering standards does not pay in the long run

"But this is an exercise in stupidity" is a complaint voiced by many in Greece and elsewhere. So it is, but so what?

DISPARAGING "Big Brother", "Bar," the "Survivor" series, and reality shows in general has been for years the favourite pastime of assorted TV reviewers, columnists, disgruntled intellectuals, neo-orthodox publicists, paleo-orthodox churchmen and even Archbishop Christodoulos himself. The producers of these programmes can do wonders for the ego of insecure pen-pushers by serving as their whipping-boys. Take, for instance, 20 March 2002, when the then chairman - since resigned - of a body of somewhat ill-defined competences named "National Council for Radio and Television" decided to suspend broadcasting of "Big Brother" and "Bar." Thankfully, the next day the council decided to allow the shows to go on so that viewers could continue to be titillated and reviewers outraged.

Truth be told, the shows are crass, unfunny and boring. However, since some 45 percent of Greeks wish to be entertained in this way, it is inconsistent to attack the broadcasts for their content and never their viewers for their taste; inconsistent but not unheard of in Greece, where "the people" are never wrong, only misguided. The villains doing the misguiding are getting all the flak - their victims all the sympathy.

While Orwell's "Big Brother" was a snooping tyrant who watched over millions of his subjects, his modern descendant is just a show where millions of voyeurs watch a bunch of pathetic volunteers making fools of themselves. Born in the Netherlands, this show has by now sunk without trace in its country of origin. It was virtually ignored by informed (as distinct from public) opinion in most of the 21 countries where it was shown since. In Britain, when the number of those voting for the final winner exceeded that of the Tory electorate, some papers even suggested that direct democracy might, after all, have its uses.

"But this is an exercise in stupidity" is a complaint voiced by many in Greece and elsewhere. So it is, but so what? Being stupid is not that uncommon, while acting stupid, at one time or another, is a universal trait of the human race. With so much of it in the air, some of it is bound to find its way on the air. An American philosopher, Avital Ronell, explores in her recent 386-page book entitled "Stupidity" the process by which humans fall short of the norms defining rational thought and behaviour. Unfortunately, the critics of "Big Brother" do not so much vituperate against its inherent imbecility as against its triviality. Their implied alternative model is that of high culture and elevated thinking. As for the show's religious opponents, these would, if they had their way, sentence viewers to endless repetitions of their monological injunctions against any kind of pleasure. A Good Christian - the theologian Prof Yannaras keeps reminding his *Kathimerini* readers on Sundays - must never stop pondering on his/her mortality.

There is no need for false dilemmas, though. TV programmes can be popular and intelligent. Take for instance the life and times of that hyperactive, seemingly dysfunctional, animated family, "The Simpsons", one of the most consistently funny and original American TV productions that has been running for years and years. With its tongue-in-cheek but true-to-life dialogue, the delightful and credible inanity of its main characters, its vertiginous pace in terms of mood change, wit, imagination and comic ruthlessness, "The Simpsons" may have incurred the disapproval of President Bush's father but they have endeared themselves to millions of viewers of all ages in the US and the world.

Such things happen in Greece too, up to a point. Mitsikostas, for instance, is a gifted impersonator who would gain greatly by avoiding his sudden lapses into vulgarity that do not become him anyway. On the other hand, an unassuming - at first glance - programme like "*S' agapo - m'agapas*" ("I Love you - you love me"), although unsophisticated and of a very traditional format, was consistently hilarious, thanks to its excellent acting, sparkling dialogue, fluent and idiomatic use of modern Greek "as she is spoke" and its underlying, commonsensical, hedonistic approach to living in Athens in the twenty first century.

TV in Greece and elsewhere may occasionally produce trash to improve ratings but this is neither mandatory nor profitable in the long run: Trash has proven to be an eminently perishable commodity.

Searching for the 'embedded' truth

One should deal with TV reports in the same way one deals with sense data - process them carefully, classify them, compare them and use one's judgment to make sense of them

THE WAY that the war in Iraq and its bloody aftermath has been reported so far has brought to the fore an age-old problem concerning truth. If, indeed, "truth is the first casualty of war", as the cliché goes, this means, at the very least, that truth is indeed a concept – and as such qualifies to be included amongst the casualties - and not a fiction, given that all reports on events are equally valid "narratives", as some post-modernists would have it. People may disagree about what is true, but that does not mean that truth is relative to perspective, that it is in the eye of the beholder and that "anything goes".

This columnist, based in London, does not have continuous access to Greek TV and is thus spared the blatant bias that its reporting is said to contain. However, by the same token, he is deprived of the hope that if only this bias were to go, the true picture of the conflict would somehow emerge. As it is, his access to a multiplicity of channels (American, British, French, et al) has only shown once again that truth is not only the opposite of lie (wilful distortion of facts or bias) but also of unconscious error, misperception and wishful thinking whose causes are many and varied.

There were many stories and many denials when the Iraq war broke out. On day one, Saddam was a target but was he killed? Yes, no, maybe, probably not - a German expert opined that the Saddam we saw the next day was 98 percent genuine. Those who had trouble with Saddam's doubles had to accept at some point that he managed to survive. Now that he is safely in prison the speculation is over, but at the time there was much confusion.

There was uncertainty about other military operations as well. The city of Umm Qasr had been taken said one channel, no, it had been secured said another, actually, it was under control said yet another. At least the viewers got a free lesson in the subtle nuances that military language is capable of. The Iraqi 51st Division has surrendered - no, it hasn't. Tariq Aziz, No 2 in the regime, has defected to the West - no, he hasn't. There was an uprising in Basra - no, there wasn't. The regime was crumbling - no, it wasn't. An Iraqi general has been captured - let's not exaggerate, he was only a colonel. Two British prisoners had been executed - no they hadn't. Tony Blair, who said so, had to breakfast on humble pie.

To top it all the WMDs (weapons of mass destruction) were there but not yet discovered, well, about to be discovered, or rather laboratories were found able to make them, no they were not, let's not exaggerate, the intention of building them was undeniable and anyway Saddam was a tyrant and the world is safer without him. Such assertions, allegations, semi-denials and fanciful "analyses" have been confusing and made viewers distrustful of everything, even of the true stories. As for the aftermath of this illegitimate bloody war that was launched, as is now clear, under false pretences not by the UN but by a "coalition of the willing" (of the duped would be a more apposite term), it is sad to observe that the more credible channel in terms of true reporting has been the Arabic Al Jazeera.

The good news is that TV has not, after all, been "weaponised". There is so much coverage and from so many angles that the viewer can quickly learn to use judgement to see through the verbiage, the wishful thinking, the hyperbole and the particular bees that some have under their bonnets. Mr Feimut Duve, senior representative of the Organisation for Security and Co-operation in Europe condemned TV coverage of the Iraqi conflict as "war entertainment". Too harsh perhaps, but not inexplicable.

So what should a viewer try to do to acquire "the correct description of an independent reality", according to one definition of the truth? Let me rephrase this question for those who will challenge the use of the term "correct" and the concept of "independent reality" as too controversial to be used in a definition. Well, how about using the only slightly more complex Kantian notion of "truth in a phenomenal world that is the joint product of things in themselves and the organising conceptual activity of the mind"? The practical problem then is how to overcome the cognitive risks of either rejecting all one hears and thus opt to remain uninformed so as not to be misinformed or, on the other hand, accept everything at face value even if this makes little sense sometimes.

The first option is suited to hermits, not citizens, and is therefore to be rejected outright. The second option is not mandatory either. One should deal with TV reports in the same way one deals with sense data

- process them carefully, classify them, compare them and use one's judgement to make sense of them.

There is even a respectable philosophical school that justifies such a practical approach to the use of information: it is known by the slightly rebarbative name of fallibilism, of which the American philosopher CS Pierce was the first exponent. A compromise between scepticism and dogmatism, this view holds that "true beliefs" based on facts do not have to be established as certain beyond the possibility of doubt. A fallibilist considers that it is sufficient - and perhaps all that is possible for human beings - for our beliefs to be treated as true if they are reasonably well-supported by our experiential evidence.

Such a critical approach making use of the "organising conceptual activity of the mind" will help us treat the TV reporting of the war in Iraq as a source of information and not entertainment.

V) Prevalent corruption ensures there is always hope for the wicked

CRONYISM is chronic in Greece, a country where malpractice is seldom punished and maladministration endemic. The buck stops nowhere, as no one is ever accountable for allowing corruption to vitiate competition – the foundation of a free market. While in western countries the government falls like a tonne of bricks on the crooks who cook the books, in Greece it often used to stand by, sometimes even as a participant observer. While the problem is now at least fully acknowledged and steps are taken to eradicate it, the time has perhaps come for Greeks to set up an NGO to fight the curse of corruption that has been stalking the land for so long.

The state we are in

Greece is run by a fistful of able patriots working hard in the state machinery to deliver the goods, without being compelled or even expected to do so. Their number does not exceed 2 percent of public servants

THE MAN in his fifties waited patiently at the MP's surgery. When his turn came, he became agitated. "Listen to me please!" he said. "I have a son in his early twenties who has just completed his military service, has no university degree, no qualifications and no job. I know that your word counts with the government and the party. So please make sure that he is appointed somewhere near us and you can rest assured that all the members of our extended family ("*Soi*" is the Greek word he used) will vote for you again at the next elections."

The MP took some notes and told the man to come back in a week's time. Their second encounter was revealing. "I have two options for your son," he told his interlocutor. "He can work as a night watchman in a factory owned by one of my friends very near here, or he can enrol in a training programme organised by the government and financed by the EU that will help him find a good job afterwards. Which do you think he would prefer?"

The man looked at him aghast. "I did not ask you for work, I asked for an APPOINTMENT," he shouted and left the room forthwith.

The man was so right. Even the Bank of Greece said so in its Economic Bulletin published on 30 July 2003. According to a study by its team of experts, men employed in the public sector earned on average - wait for it - 34 percent more than men of comparable experience and qualifications in the private sector. Women have it even better, as for them the disparity reaches 37 percent. Interestingly, there are changes in the comparative pay structure as public servants' careers unfold. Entry-level wages are 48 percent higher in the public sector, "falling" to only 24 percent higher at director level. The man was right. His son should be appointed to serve the state, not trained to satisfy the market, be paid less and live in constant threat of losing his job.

Is there an underside to the advantages accruing to civil servants and achieved through the "struggles" of state trade unions? Only that appointees will have to work (the term should be interpreted loosely) with and under the supervision of persons who think they are too clever by half, but really too stupid (and/or venal) by three-quarters. It is not just the salary, though. There are also incentives in the guise of "productivity bonuses". These started originally at the ministry of education and were initially meant to be individual awards to those who would toil over and above the call of duty. This, however, would create inequalities, with some civil servants earning more than their colleagues of the same rank and equal number of years in service. So the unions mobilised and struck to achieve "equality". As a result, productivity bonuses are now awarded to all and sundry, irrespective of performance. Meritocracy did rear its ugly head once in the Greek civil service but not for long.

So how do these well-paid, pampered employees enjoying full security of tenure actually perform? A study by the European Central Bank by Antonio Afonso, Lufger Schuknecht and Vito Tanzi entitled "Public Sector Efficiency: An International Comparison" made public on July 16, 2003 ranked Greece last among 23 developed countries. The top four positions were taken by Luxembourg, Japan, the Netherlands and Austria. The study calculated that if those employed in Greece's public administration were paid the market price for the services they actually offered, their cost to the budget would be 27 percent lower than it is today. So Greek taxpayers overpay in return for lousy service.

The general conclusion of this study was that countries with "small government" (absorbing less than 40 percent of GDP) were more efficient than those like Greece, who spend more than 50 percent of their GDP, mostly on their civil servants. Mr Karamanlis who is now in charge of this placid, avid and slow-moving Leviathan has pledged to "refound" the Greek state and make it work better. He was successful in convincing the electorate to welcome this promise with the pulse-pounding, page-turning, sphincter-tightening feeling of tremulous expectation that ensured him a decisive victory at the polls. Fine. However, he now finds that his own trade unionists who have contributed to create the state we are in are up in arms against him not because he has not as yet even started "refounding" the state but because his ministers are not giving them their share of the spoils. In this they are aided and abetted by the party's organisations demanding noisily that their offspring be appointed forthwith here and now in the public sector, of course.

There is a silver lining to this cloud. Greece is run by a fistful of able patriots working hard in the state machinery to deliver the goods, without being compelled or even expected to do so. This columnist has it on good authority that their number does not exceed 2 percent of the total. To add a word of caution: this percentage applies also to the armed forces and the police.

In Greece, the buck stops nowhere

*The suicide note of finance ministry real-estate official
Roubini Stathea is an eloquent, poignant, indictment of
how the Greek system works (or doesn't)*

WHEN Tony Blair was asked, point blank, in Japan in September
2003 "Mr Prime Minister, do you have blood on your hands?" he
mumbled something and changed the subject. However, Mr Blair could
have invoked in connection with Dr Kelly's suicide the presumption of
innocence until the well-run Hutton enquiry had published its findings.
Shouldn't someone have asked Mr Costas Simitis, the same question a
month later? The suicide of Rubini Stathea, assistant director in the
finance ministry's real-estate department, shook Greek public opinion
for months after her body was found at the bottom of a 20-metre cliff
near Keratea around 6pm on Sunday 12 October 2003. There was, of
course, no chance of the Greek premier ordering anything like the
Hutton enquiry with its attendant publicity and courageous scrutiny of
the ways bureaucracy crushes its victims. One could only hope that the
prosecutor dealing with the case would be up to the task.

The deceased would not be so sure. Even though, or perhaps
because, her suicide note was such an understatement - a word,
incidentally, that has no equivalent in the Modern Greek language - it
became an eloquent, poignant, indictment of how the Greek system
works (or doesn't). "I wish," she wrote "that my end may mark the
beginning of a small effort by all to become better. The civil servants a
little more industrious, responsible and efficient; the politicians a little
more honest; the members of the judiciary a little more credible; the
journalists a little less carnivorous." The poor woman was crucified by
the press for having reversed more than once her decisions on whether
some buildings in Lagonissi belonging to Greek tycoons should be pulled
down as illegal or not.

Now, this issue of buildings erected without planning permission -
routinely legitimised before each general election - defies logic altogether.
For one thing, there is no unambiguous way of establishing whether a
building is or is not illegal at any given moment. The illegality of a
building in Greece, is like treason - as somebody once said (Talleyrand
probably) - mostly a question of timing. That is why it is imperative for

the trespassers to avoid implementation of any adverse decisions at least until the next general election when their sins will be forgiven in exchange for their expected voting behaviour. The press mentioned recently cases of final, unappealable court decisions that have not been implemented for five whole years! The number of agencies, authorities and persons that have a legitimate say in the matter is quite impressive. This plethora makes them cancel each other out so that nothing happens The beleaguered civil servant, like Rubini Stathea, has to grapple with a multitude of contradictory laws, arbitrary interpretations of such laws, innumerable regulations and a rich variety of procedural devices for delaying the implementation of decisions that have been supposedly finalised. Add to that the daily burden of aggressive lobbying and pressures from all sides and it is no wonder that (s)he soon gets so hopelessly enmeshed in a spider's web of intrigue and countermanded orders that (s)he reaches the end of his/her tether.

There comes a point when the five rules of survival within the Greek bureaucracy cease to apply. These are:

1) Don't think
2) If you do think, don't speak
3) I you do think and speak, don't write
4) If you think, speak and write, don't sign
5) If you think, speak, write and sign, don't be surprised.

Rubini Stathea - married, two children - was not surprised. She simply had had enough and could take no more. So she took her life. Who, then, has her blood on his hands? The tragedy is that, in pure bureaucratic tradition there is no indubitable answer to this either.

Fifty-eight years ago, almost to the day of the poor woman's self-sacrifice, on 2 October 1945, president Harry Truman put on his desk a painted glass sign mounted on a walnut base reading "The Buck Stops Here". This was an expression of Missouri poker players referring to a marker - or even a knife with a buckhorn handle in the frontier days - that was used to indicate the person whose turn it was to deal. If the player did not want to do so, he passed the "buck", as it came to be known, to someone else. "Pass the buck" first appeared in poker jargon around 1865 and has been used in the figurative sense of "passing responsibility to someone else" since 1900. The meaning Harry Truman gave to this slogan, which he used many times in his speeches, was that he intended to accept the ultimate responsibility for any actions by his administrators.

In Greece, alas, "The Buck Stops Here" - or any ancient Greek equivalent of the saying - has never been on anybody's desk. This is because in Greece the buck stops nowhere. It runs and runs, up and down; it runs about; it runs in circles; it runs aground; and finally it runs out. Responsibility evaporates.

Perhaps Greek officials ought to display on their desks a sign reading not "The Buck Stops Here" but "The f*** starts here". This would at least act as a warning...

Corruption is bad for business

A number of people in Greece still see capitalism in Marxist-Leninist terms as an inherently unstable system ruled by the frenetic pursuit of profit. This is utterly wrong

NEARLY two decades ago, the late Agamemnon Koutsogiorgas – vice-premier, in charge of Greece when Andreas Papandreou was unwell - argued that the judiciary should tread very carefully in the case against Koskotas - a banker who had swindled 35 billion drachmas from the Bank of Crete that he was "managing" - because this "might damage the Greek banking system". To be on the safe side, Koskotas paid Koutsogiorgas two million dollars into a Swiss bank account to have a law voted in parliament that would exonerate him. The arrangement fell through but not for lack of trying by any of the parties involved.

The trouble is and was that a number of people in Greece still see capitalism in Marxist-Leninist terms as an inherently unstable system ruled by the frenetic pursuit of profit. This is utterly wrong. The central tenet of capitalism that distinguishes it from all other systems is not the pursuit of profit but the strict enforcement of the rules of competition. Abolish competition through corrupt practices, and you abolish the free market because corrupt businessmen do not make their profits by selling competitively priced products of good quality but thanks to their privileged access to the state's power and coffers through political manipulation, bribery, nepotism, cronyism and other forms of favouritism.

This is not a new discovery. Adam Smith said of those who tried to form monopolies at the expense of the public: "People of the same trade seldom meet together even for merriment and diversion, but the conversation ends in a conspiracy against the public, or in some contrivance to raise prices" ("Wealth of Nations", book 1, ch.2). Left to themselves, producers will be strongly tempted to give consumers a rough deal. That is why even giant Microsoft has to defend itself against accusations of monopolistic practices and why the American political and judicial authorities have fallen on Enron like a tonne of bricks. US capitalism, is implacable against capitalists who attempt to undermine its very foundation, i.e. free competition.

So Mr Kokkalis, for instance, who is now again under investigation for a great variety of alleged financial crimes, must not be allowed to wriggle his way out of a fair and thorough examination of his record. He must be given all the guarantees of a fair trial but no favours whatsoever because of friends in high places, or even in low places as the owner of a popular football team that is dubbed in Greek *o thrylos* (the legend).

One would have hoped to have heard an unambiguous condemnation by the then government of the corrupt system that led poor Rubini Stathea to take her life. It had plenty of opportunities to do so as it was under almost daily attack by New Democracy, then in the opposition, for innumerable cases of corruption in all walks of public life. Instead, the former prime minister Mr Simitis preferred to indulge in incomprehensibly alarmist speeches against unidentified conspiracies and unnamed forces allegedly bent on bringing down his government and the democratic system. The two are, of course, unconnected (governments are regularly brought down in stable parliamentary democracies) and neither has anything to do with what happens to the practical abolition of the rule of law when it comes to illegal house building to take just one case.

Stability ought perhaps to be (re)defined in Greece. It is not a state of bliss without problems but a state of activity where problems are solved within, by and through the democratic institutions in place.

Empowering citizens in the fight against corruption

Modern Greeks like to condemn clientelism collectively while many amongst them strive to benefit from it individually

THE POLICE officer was jubilant but also somewhat apprehensive. He had just arrested an important figure of the underworld in flagrante while he was selling a large shipment of heroin. The captive offered no resistance but asked his captor to allow him to make a phone call on his mobile.

This was granted. He spoke softly and then handed the apparatus to the startled policeman. "He wants to speak to you," he said. Curious, the officer took the phone and heard the soothing voice of a notorious "godfather" asking him whether the gift of a new luxury car could convince him to allow the arrested person to "escape" with his "merchandise".

The answer was a firm "no". The man was taken to the police station. Within an hour, he was released without charge. His parting words to his captor were: "What a pity. You would now have had your Mercedes and everything would have been fine. Now my boss had to pay your boss much more!"

This incident did not take place in Athens, but in Moscow. Nevertheless, there is little room for complacency because policemen in Greece have been caught robbing banks, running extortion rackets and selling protection to prostitution gangs. Even the Internal Affairs Department, created by the hard-nosed former public order minister Michalis Chrysohoidis, has had its share of black sheep to cope with.

The past couple of years of debate in parliament about corruption have not been as bad, futile and inconsequential as they might appear. There are differences in emphasis and attempts to change the subject but the truth is that nobody tries to justify corruption. Nobody dismisses it as a "necessary evil" or attempts to explain it away as Mrs Gandhi is said to have done once by calling bribery of officials "a parallel taxation system". Up till now, though, stigmatising the Greek politicians' habit of buying votes in exchange for favours was mostly left to Greek academics and the odd newspaper columnist.

There is nothing new, alas, in this. The roots of cronyism go deep in

Greece. Modern Greeks like to vituperate collectively against obsequiousness, patronage, manipulation and cringe - called in Greek *rousfeti* (clientelism) by its Arabic name - while many amongst them strive to benefit from it individually.

The ancient Greeks were no better even if some members of their elite were. In a book published in 1999 under the euphemistic title "Reciprocity in Ancient Greece", 14 scholars show convincingly that cronyism has always been a major threat to impartiality, accountability and democracy in the ancient polis.

Some of the essays make fascinating reading. There is, for instance, Ephialtes, one of the champions of Athenian democracy, who turned down a donation of 10 talents from his friends so as not to be beholden to them. There is also good old Pericles, who "did not attend a single friend's house for dinner during the long period of his political involvement". Then there is Creon, who upon deciding to go into politics "renounced all his friendships as something which often weakens and perverts the just choice of policy..."

Stern stuff that most of today's politicians obsessed with the cult of "parea" (gang of buddies) have little time for.

Maybe, however, the time has come for Greeks to stop complaining and start acting against the widespread institutionalised corruption that is plaguing the country. Such action requires an initiative to be taken by the government. Here then is a suggestion for the present government of New Democracy. This is – to remind you dear reader – a ruling party dedicated to fight *rousfeti* no matter what the political cost even if it means putting down rebellions such as the recent one by its outraged rank and file suffering from "withdrawal of favours" symptoms. The justice ministry could and should install a hotline for the public to denounce acts of corruption, just as the public order ministry did to collect information about terrorism.

Trained personnel should man the phones, record the calls and manage not to be swamped by the sheer number of denunciations (many of them bogus) they will receive. A competent back office should then process the information and liaise for any follow-up with the police, the internal revenue and all appropriate authorities. Anonymous calls should, of course, be welcome. Successes of the system should be given the widest possible publicity to encourage citizens to come forward with their complaints.

Short of such a government initiative, and until such time as this is set up properly and has had its test-run, here is another suggestion worth considering. An NGO composed of persons of known integrity, competence and dedication to the fight against corruption in Greece could and should be set up as soon as possible and appeal to citizens for support and funding. Under good leadership, such a body could do wonders. The prize is of some value. "Among a people generally corrupt," wrote Edmund Burke in 1777 to the Sheriffs of Bristol, "liberty cannot long exist."

VI) Greek political parties struggling to differ

U nder Simitis, the ruling party, PASOK, changed its image as a traditional socialist "mummy" party (caring, solicitous, populist) that spared the rod and spoiled the voter into that of a purposeful career woman keen (but not always succeeding) to see her children become achievers in a competitive world. As a result, PASOK became the root of all troubles for PASOK. Successive reshuffles that led nowhere only confirmed many Greeks' conviction that the time had come for Simitis to put PASOK out of its misery by creating another party or sink with it at the next election, which is exactly what happened. Meanwhile New Democracy, having offered a diagnosis and prescribed a treatment to make the broadly common policies work, convinced the electorate that it could also implement the cure. It has started doing so but with extreme caution – dictated in part by lingering populist tendencies within the party – and with a tendency to shift the blame to its predecessors whenever it finds itself in difficulties.

A sex change in Greek politics?

Governments in Greece have by now been developing more like an assertive career woman, or a 'caring' father, as distinctions between Leftist 'mummy' and Rightist 'daddy' parties have been blurring

RIGHT after the Second World War, the freshly constituted United Nations tied itself in knots over the issue of human rights. The West favoured the so-called "negative freedoms", such as the right not to be tortured under any circumstances, not to be persecuted for one's opinions and not to be thwarted in the pursuit of one's lawful activities. These political and civic rights, first proclaimed by the French Revolution, were not to the liking of the Soviet Union and its satellites. Communists throughout the world championed the so-called "social rights," stipulating that humans have the right to health, food, education, shelter, employment and much else besides.

To use Isaiah Berlin's classic distinction, the first set of rights comes under the heading "freedom from" (persecution) while the second is an instance of "freedom to" (enjoy a decent standard of living). The former is ensured by a state of law the latter can only be implemented by a welfare state disposing of the necessary means. Lacking anything approaching universal legal support, these "social rights" are routinely flouted in all corners of the world.

Communism has collapsed but the conceptual divide on "rights" has not disappeared. It has marked democratic politics throughout the world. The Right - especially under its Liberal guise - has, broadly speaking, emphasised freedom from coercion and the values that go with it, i.e. private initiative, enterprise, creativity, productivity and individual responsibility. The Left – whether socialist, social-democratic or centre-left – has promoted the values of solidarity, free public services and the creation of an adequate welfare state. In other words, the Left has been predominantly the "mummy party" (caring, solicitous, all-embracing) while the Right or "daddy party" has insisted on the person's optimal use of his/her freedom to achieve self-reliance.

This distinction has now been blurred somewhat. President Bush paid lip service in 2000 when he was first elected to something he then called "compassionate conservatism". He has not repeated it after being re-elected for a second term in 2004, but he has not repudiated it either. On the other hand, the leader of the British Labour party, Prime Minister Tony Blair has adopted former conservative Mrs Thatcher's remark about the Good Samaritan who could be charitable only because he had money to spare. In Greece too, the "mummy party" changed under Premier Costas Simitis, who abandoned resolutely Andreas Papandreou's policies of wealth distribution and supreme disdain of wealth creation promoted by the hated Establishment.

Under Simitis, mummy was no longer the irresponsible female of Andreas Papandreou's time who spared the rod and spoiled the child, plunging the country into debt and spending her husband's hard-earned cash. Under Simitis, "mummy" evolved into a purposeful, thoughtful European career woman, who wants her children to succeed in life, praises them for their achievements, scolds them for their mistakes and allocates as much as she can from the household coffers to their welfare without courting bankruptcy. George Papandreou who only bears a physical resemblance to his father is basically of the same view with the difference that he wants the children to do much more than just vote for him. He wants them to learn how to make decisions on their own, use the internet judiciously and follow the rules, having first understood and accepted them. He is no socialist, and even tried at some point to rename PASOK by omitting any mention of "socialism" but was not allowed to do so by his dinosaurian colleagues who would fight to the finish to preserve their natural habitat unchanged.

Meanwhile, New Democracy, the centre-right "daddy party" created by Constantine Karamanlis senior – both in the sense of wealth creation and paternalism – has also undergone a sex change. When it was in the opposition, Costas Karamanlis junior even allowed himself to oppose some of Simitis' policies (on privatisations, for instance) that he knew made sense. This is a well-known symptom afflicting parties sitting on the opposition benches. The Earl of Derby even proclaimed it as a principle when he said in the House of Commons in 1841: "The duty of an Opposition is very simple: to oppose everything and propose nothing." Once in government, however, daddy softened his policies. In his speech at the International Trade Fair in Thessaloniki in September 2004 Karamanlis junior defined precisely the new version of his "daddy party" policies: "We are creating a competitiveness umbrella," he said, "that will spread out to cover all activities in the public and private sectors. We are promoting a quality revolution in the provision of goods and services. The basic goal of our policy is to increase wealth and distribute it more fairly."

When a political party, any party, has its clothes stolen by a rival party, it not only risks going beyond transvestism and suffering a sex change but also makes everyone become aware of it. Now that both of Greece's major parties have exchanged clothes there is at least a consensus emerging on fundamentals. There are good reasons to hope that from now on any promises of "change" will refer to implementation only.

The Sisyphean socialist governance of Greece

PASOK lost the 2004 elections because of...PASOK. Simitis could only have won them if he had changed his party into something entirely different and himself into a credible liberal politician

TRUTH does not always come out of the mouth of babes. Occasionally, it comes out of the mouth of law enforcers. Witness the senior police officer who had this to say to *Kathimerini* (20 June 2002) on the shooting incident outside the prime minister's residence on 9 June 2002: "We feel like Sisyphus pushing a rock to a mountain peak and just before we get there something happens and the rock hurtles back down so that we have to start all over again." There is a difference, though, between the ancient Greeks who used the Sisyphus myth as a prescription of what to avoid and the modern ones who use it as a description of what happens.

Sisyphus has not always been working work full-time in Greece. Even allowing for PASOK's blunders, the "fundamentals" to use the current jargon, have not been too bad this millennium. Inflation has been kept reasonably under control, growth has been vigorous, the Olympic projects were completed on time and some social services have somewhat improved, even if corruption levels, nepotism and waste have been kept consistently high.

The same happened in France, where the socialists got the fundamentals more or less right under Lionel Jospin, also a charmless, personally honest, professorial type, and yet failed dismally to impress the electorate. So, one may well wonder, why do voters vote to fix a machine that ain't broke? The answer is that what they are missing is hope. Hope for a new departure a brighter tomorrow, more honest governance, less routine incompetence, sleaze and empty rhetoric.

PASOK suffered from having been in government far too long for its own good and from having been left unreconstructed by a "modernising" management that was granted eight long years to show its mettle and didn't. Simitis pushed his comrades kicking and screaming into the eurozone, forcing them through a systematic detoxification programme, weaning them off, for a while, from their addiction to using public funds for partisan purposes. The withdrawal symptoms remained serious throughout. During the last days of the PASOKian Pompei, while the popular volcano was on the verge of erupting and its grandees more or less realised that their days in office were numbered, all knives came out in a Hobbesian war of all against all. PASOK lost the 2004 elections because of...PASOK. Simitis could only have won them if he had changed his party into something entirely different and himself into a credible liberal politician This he was unable (or unwilling) to do, so things got worse. When street protests, mainly on behalf of a bloated public sector, can threaten the government because the protesters can count on the support of many an MP of the governing party, as happened repeatedly during Simitis' second term, voters turn away from it in droves, as one opinion poll after the other confirmed again and again.

No electorate in the world likes its government being blackmailed and coerced to make policy on the hoof under the pressure of lobbies, unions and factions within the governing party. Simitis was shrewd enough to realise this, and he made sure that somebody else paid the price of the party's progressive collapse into irrelevance. Its new leader will have a huge task reforming a party in denial that seems to have sunk into a perpetual lamentation mode.

For PASOK to become once again a party of government, it would have to achieve the transition from the old, protective, redistributive, heavily partisan and populist model of governance created by Andreas Papandreou, to a modern, meritocratic, honest, efficient and impartial one that will not attempt to rob Peter to pay Paul but will protect them both from unfair treatment and maladministration, giving them a chance to do their own thing, choose their own ways and means, ends and values, goals and targets within the law.

New Democracy has adopted such a model proclaiming - not too loudly, one must admit - that it is no longer an old-style orthodox conservative, clientelistic, paternalistic, nationalistic party of the "popular Right", but a modern liberal party with the necessary oomph to lift all obstacles to an explosion of investment in Greece, to maximise opportunities for all Greeks (and not just for its supporters), and to protect them from criminal activities, corruption and discrimination in all walks of life.

Those who voted it into power on 7 March 2004 should be both willing and able to hold their new rulers constantly to account. A healthy mistrust of politicians and a government held under scrutiny by an informed public and an inquisitive press will serve Greece well after the

"PASOK experience". The proclaimed good intentions of any government should never again suffice for granting it a blank cheque. That is the way to put poor Sisyphus to rest, bless his soul.

Is the party over?

If there is somebody who thinks that there is unused PASOK talent which, given half a chance, could turn the tables in favour of the party and make it electable again (s)he has not yet surfaced

A NDREAS Papandreou used to reshuffle his cabinet every six months or so, because he was afraid that a long-lasting minister might one day overshadow him. Only the late Melina Mercouri was more or less permanent because she had never been any danger to anyone.

Keen, however, to distinguish himself from his conservative predecessors, the founder of PASOK renamed the changes to his cabinet – which he never consulted anyway – by the fancy term "restructuring" (*αναδόμηση*). This allowed him to claim a biannual "new beginning" for the ruling party even though recycling the same tired old faces signalled that there was simply "no end" to the process.

Simitis proved different. For one thing, he never felt insecure. Unlike Andreas Papandreou who was never sure of the loyalty of his followers, because only he knew how much he had lied to them, Simitis had a much more stable concept of his own worth and integrity. He granted his ministers ample time and margin to prove their worth or make fools of themselves - a right that some of them exercised to the best of their inability. At some point, however, during the last year of his rule he started facing a quandary as even his trusted lieutenants started getting thrown overboard at the rate of one or two a month, accused of sleaze, personal enrichment and "unsocialist" behaviour. To counter this, he spread the word widely that he was preparing "something big" during his last year in power. Greeks were led to believe that "a page would be turned", and that, at long last, the prospect of honest and competent governance by PASOK would bring back to the fold all the disgruntled supporters of the government that kept telling opinion pollsters they would vote for New Democracy in the next elections.

As it happened, under Simitis, the cabinet was never as much as shuffled as modestly rearranged. The same continues to happen after the party changed its leader, with the difference that having lost the elections there is no cabinet any longer, only a political bureau whose very existence is in the balance. If there is somebody who thinks that there is unused PASOK talent which, given half a chance, could turn the tables in favour of the party and make it electable again (s)he has not yet surfaced. If there are any outsiders who could be groomed to become, sometime in the future, cabinet material, they have not given so far an inkling of their presence. The new leader, George Papandreou, is in desperate need of competent and incorrupt people who might convince the voters that he will not stand alone forever, presiding over a party that is, at present, as fluid as a loose company of friends, as disciplined as an NGO and as committed to political activism as the participants in an Internet chat-room.

In fact, in his difficulty in finding an effective team, he has come up against the problem described in the sad little ditty by Elisabeth Wordsworth who died in 1932.

If all the good people were clever,
And all the clever people were good.
The world would be better that ever,
We thought it possible could.
But alas it is seldom or never,
That things will turn out as they should.

The sad truth for PASOK has been that, at its twilight, voters no longer judged it on its merits, which were considerable in the year 2003: a successful EU presidency, a reasonable relationship with Turkey, Cyprus' EU membership, a deadly blow against the sinister 17N terrorists, fairly competent preparation of the 2004 Olympics and a good rate of growth, even if too dependent on outside factors. Voters have simply had enough of PASOK, the posturing of its leading members, the stuffy grandiloquent language they used, their bottomless hypocrisy, the perceived corruption of some, their invocation of conspiracies to explain failure away, and at the last months of their rule, their manifest panic at the prospect of losing power.

The task, then, for Simitis during the sunset months of the party was not to dream the impossible dream of a sudden regeneration but to manage his party's retreat in a dignified way. He did this as best he could. First, he gave the ring of party power (but not of government) to George Papandreou and, second, he resisted as best he could his comrades' pressures to spend, spend, spend in order to buy favour with the electorate.

As for ND, it came to power because voters were justifiably attracted by its promises to free Greece from the incubuses of populism, favouritism and anti-meritocratic policies. Some sceptics maintained that these promises were too good to be fulfilled and that after its victory, New Democracy would be trying to satisfy all and sundry, proclaiming that "everybody has won and all must have prizes". This, however, was Dodo's verdict on the caucus race in "Alice's Adventures in Wonderland" - hardly suitable as a motto for a modern liberal party. The sceptics were not vindicated, and, as opinion polls have been showing, the new government has acquired a solid reputation of honesty and truthfulness. This is good provided it lasts

Today's New Democracy government should never forget that during all these years under PASOK's rule, the Greek voters have become experts in reading between the lies.

What PASOK really needs, is euthanasia and a decent burial

Will George Papandreou ever have the guts to put PASOK out of its misery and create a new party in name also?

THE LAST ever of PASOK's reshuffles in the summer of 2003 was a sham. Like a pantomime without the jokes, five deputy ministers were wheeled out and five wheeled in, one from the left and one from the right wing of the theatre. Exeunt some figures to be dumped on a heap ready for a comeback when booty calls. Enter some new ones useful to push the leadership's policies down the throats of the Old PASOK diehards. So what else is new?

It was slightly unfair to blame Simitis for the reshuffle that never was. He had little choice. He could not replace key ministers nine months before the elections and expect the new ones to outperform their predecessors in that time. So he decided to don his best head-masterly style and make the ones he was saddled with work better. This proved difficult, as all of them had started their campaign to get re-elected, a resources-consuming activity especially when opinion polls are inclement and competition for a shrinking number of parliamentary seats becomes that much fiercer. For all these reasons, Simitis opted for a comic opera reshuffle where grandiloquence presaging the action is out of kilter with the unfolding action itself. He nourished the legitimate hope that by convincing his team - such as it was - to do little things well, they might collectively end up able to claim that they had done big things better.

By making incremental changes to his cabinet and pretending that they were earth-shattering, Simitis admitted, of course, that the crisis in governance that had necessitated them was not, after all, the result of a conspiracy - as he had claimed - but a case of routine incompetence pure and simple.

Simitis knew that the elections he eventually lost would not be fought over his record - which was not too bad especially compared to the disastrous performance of his predecessor, Andreas Papandreou. In a democracy, votes are not awarded like medals; they are cast on expectations as even Winston Churchill found out when he lost the elections after the war. To raise expectations for real change Simitis got rid of Laliotis, PASOK's secretary, replacing him with Mr Michalis

Chrysochoidis, who had cut his teeth as public order minister. The man had showed himself to be a modest workaholic blessed with a laser-beam capacity of focusing on the targets he had set himself (such as dismantling the sinister 17 November gang). It was he who had taken the bull by the horns in 2002 when he suggested that PASOK change its name, its symbols and its orientation. His proposal was then ignored rather than refuted.

Let us then start with the name.

The Panhellenic Socialist Movement has always been something of a misnomer that turned into a myth that became an albatross around Simitis' neck and that George Papandreou attempted in vain to get rid off – when he assumed the leadership – by diluting it, to start with, into a suitably vague Grand Democratic Camp (Megali Dimokratiki Parataxi). The "Panhellenic" bit - consonant with Andreas' rhetoric - is now seen as a joke. All parties are "panhellenic", in the sense that they appeal to all Greeks, and none is, in the sense that none can aspire to command the loyalties of all Greeks. So this meaningless epithet can easily go.

As for the word "Movement" itself, this too sounds ridiculous, if vaguely menacing. It was originally chosen by Andreas in order to convey the notion of masses of Greeks busily building together a new society, not simply a group of citizens voting for a parliamentary party. Those were the days when the talk was always of masses, never of citizens, when Andreas proclaimed that "the only institution is the sovereign people". The word started to sound definitely incongruous when PASOK, as a "panhellenic" organisation, lost all capacity for movement and even approached the rigor mortis stage.

As for the word "socialist", this has by now definitely served its purpose. There are those who say - with good reason - that the word had been misleading right from the start, but let that pass. George Papandreou must now convince the voters who deserted PASOK during the last elections and are happy to have done so – as opinion polls keep showing – that he is pro-market, pro-business and, let us be blunt, pro-globalisation. The "socialist" label has therefore become a liability. So he must get rid of it. Some would say that he even left it a bit late.

Will George Papandreou ever have the guts to put PASOK out of its misery and create a new party? Getting rid of PASOK is no recipe of success but a country can only gain when its leaders decide to bury the dead with some decorum.

Shifting the blame is the name of the game

New Democracy finds itself in a quandary: it won power, won the argument and is still often at a loss what to do with some of its own people

GREEK domestic politics tend to become the art of the impossible. Take, for instance, the case of the Athens Stock Exchange. Five years ago, in mid-March 2000, when prices tumbled, investors blamed the government and so did, at the time, New Democracy. They wanted the government to raise share prices and, absurdly, the government to keep its hands off the market when it is bullish and give a helping hand to the losers when it is bearish.

In 2003,as the country entered an extended electoral period, ND leader Costas Karamanlis presented himself as the protector of the "trapped ones" (εγκλωβισμένοι). This is a term that applies both to the few Greeks living on Turkish-Cypriot territory in northern Cyprus and to the investors who have witnessed the prices of their shares lose 70-80 percent of their value, still clinging to them in the hope that, one day, they will once again rise. Their champion has been all along a sad figure in ND by the name of Miltiades Evert, a former leader of the party and representative of the so-called "populist Right" who has been asking that those "responsible for the Athens Stock Exchange fiasco be brought to justice". Fortunately the Greek justice system dismissed the case in November 2004, found no wrongdoing by anyone and there the matter should rest. Fortunately too, the ND government did not comment on the decision, even if Mr Evert did.

This was, of course, to be expected because Karamanlis had never promised that if elected he would keep share prices going up all the time. He simply said that the previous government had interfered in the Stock Exchange with the then finance minister urging people to buy shares and gloating that under PASOK's management Greece's capital market had become vibrant. Karamanlis also promised that if elected, his party would not interfere in such matters, a self-evident truth that needed, alas, to be repeated in 21st century Greece.

The trouble is that Greek shareholders are, overall, bad losers. They want assurances that they will have their daily cake and eat it too. When their shares go up, they feel insightful, proud, clever and full of guile.

When the index goes down, they start whining, looking for scapegoats and inventing a rich variety of "conspiracies" both domestic and international to justify their mishap.

They themselves are, of course, always beyond blame as they can never be – or do – wrong. In fact, they seem to think that they are free agents only when they succeed. Otherwise, they are simply victims of a wide range of dark forces whose aims, methods and modus operandi vary according to each and every aggrieved loser. The truth is they were not alone in thinking like this. At a time when opinion polls predicted with increasing persistence that PASOK would lose the elections, shifting the blame had become second nature to the government itself. This was new because up till then PASOK had had a relatively easy ride.

The real trouble facing both parties is that a – fortunately dwindling – number of Greeks simply refuse to be modernised if that means less protection from the vagaries of the market and less security of job tenure, while meritocracy threatens to run wild in the civil service, even in the teaching profession.

The difficulty facing ND as an opposition before and as a government now is that it cannot capitalise on this resentment as PASOK did under Andreas Papandreou with such devastating panache. To fight for hypothetical "peoples' rights" without legitimising your policies with socialist rhetoric is not in the gift of your average Evert-type centre-right strategist, no matter how hard he tries to suppress liberal doctrines by promoting populist attitudes.

New Democracy has therefore to cope with some of its own die-hards still full of nostalgia for a kind of right-wing paternalism that would favour first and foremost "our boys and girls". New Democracy thus finds itself in a quandary: it won power, won the argument and is still often at a loss what to do with some of its own people.

Careful not to upset anyone, Karamanlis is thus obliged to play many roles at once: with school kids he is both compassionate and stern; with businessmen he is a free-marketeer but also in favour of state regulation "when necessary"; he shows "understanding" when addressing trade-unionists and tells them he is ready for "dialogue". Every move he makes, every step he takes, he is bound to be cautious except when he attacks his predecessors for the mess they made. They, of course, will never accept they did anything wrong and try to shift the blame to the ND government for revealing the truth about some of their shoddy manoeuvres. It is like blaming the thermometer for the fever.

Shifting the blame is not new in Greece.

In his first speech in the Odyssey (Book 1, verses 37-40, translated by Robert Fagles), Zeus exclaims:

Ah, how shameless the way these mortals blame the gods.
From us alone, they say, come all their miseries, yes.

Zeus comes across in the "Odyssey" mostly as a greedy, arrogant, vengeful and highly unpredictable god who had little time for mortals, as he nourished no illusions about them. When push came to shove, he too liked to shift the blame on them.

VII) And now for something completely different...

A columnist comments on what is and what happens. He is, therefore, entitled to muse, at times, how things have come to be; he is entitled to wonder whether modern science allows man to play God at the physical micro-level. In the same line of inquiry, he may also be tempted to ask himself whether the Resurrection of God's son – the foundation of Christianity – makes sense. Also, he might ponder whether the dual nature of Jesus (human and divine) is as problem-free as the Church maintains and whether his mother's image in Greece has always been faithful to Mary's discretion and humility as testified in the gospels.

To choose not to choose is a human prerogative

So are we really playing God at the micro-level? Are we, mere mortals, still in the business of creation in our laboratories? And what about the things that are already created, the mountains, the seas, the animals? Can we create and uncreate them at will?

THESE days it is not politicians, diplomats and the military that create shock and awe. It is the physicists. Here is what they have been saying recently on TV and the press worldwide.

Matter is no longer composed of particles, however elementary. The Universe's building blocks are tiny vibrating strings of energy, which account for what is, what attracts what is (gravity, electromagnetism, atomic forces), what accommodates what is (space) and what makes what is last (time); in fact they are the foundation for "a theory of everything". Elegant mathematical formulae give expression to this extraordinary theory, and huge tunnels are being dug to make atoms collide at speeds approaching the speed of light to provide experimental confirmation. String theorists have scored significant success in explaining the Black Holes but not that much in explaining the Big Bang. So every now and again, a professor has a go at telling us how it all started.

John Archibald Wheeler, professor at Princeton University, has put forth his own proposal. He starts from the well-known quantum theory of indeterminacy that says the properties of a subatomic particle (momentum and/or position) remain in abeyance, in a kind of fog of possibility until someone measures it or something hits it. So could the Universe somehow bootstrap itself into being when billions of potential quantum interactions suddenly converge into one world-creating Big Bang explosion? He calls this notion "genesis by observership".

Let us explore it somewhat. Here is an impious thought, a kind of 21st-century theodicy. Could the Creator really have been the Observer? Could he (or she or it) have simply glanced at the primordial soup of possibilities and by so doing have shuffled all the strings into place for the Big Bang to occur? Genesis emphasises the primacy of language in Creation even though language evolved as a purely human attribute many billion of years later. "And God said 'let there be light': and there was light" (Genesis Ch 1, v 1). It seems as if God creates things by naming them. But what if nothing was really said but everything was observed? Could that have been how it all started?

Nice try but it will not wash. Quantum theory says that here and now, just by observing, we can make particles (or strings) acquire momentum, position and other attributes of existence. So are we really playing God at the micro-level? Are we, mere mortals, still in the business of creation in our laboratories? And what about the things that are already created, the mountains, the seas, the animals? Can we create and uncreate them at will?

This is absurd. It is not even science-fantasy but simply a dream world without laws where anything can happen. It sounds daft but let us speculate further. Could existence not be an all-or-none affair? Could we have degrees of existence as we have degrees of freedom, truth, beauty, knowledge or temperature? Suppose the primordial soup of possibilities was not exhausted with the Big Bang; suppose that it still exists in some deep recesses of the Universe; suppose further that we can detect, observe and bring into being not bits of virtual reality (TV does that) but - to coin a phrase - "real virtuality"; suppose we are able, as it were, to continue on a do-it-yourself basis the job of creation in our laboratories. Would that be so unthinkable?

In fact, there is one area where this happens daily. Focusing on people's behaviour creates attitudes. The press is always wondering at the inconsistencies and contradictions found in opinion polls. How could respondents before Greece's 2004 election, for instance, both prefer Simitis to Karamanlis and New Democracy to Pasok? It happened, one might say, because a question focusing on a choice generates a position (just as it happens with electrons that also, by the way, have "degrees of freedom"), which may be at odds with positions created by other questions. The process of generating attitudes is not straightforward; gut reactions are not reasoned views. Moreover, opinion polls show vividly how shedding light on a variety of choices makes some respondents retreat into the safety of indeterminacy. The Don't Knows find comfort in the soup of possibilities where they can swim freely without strings attached. Unlike the strings of energy that they are made of, humans like sometimes to choose not to choose, or at least not to reveal their choices.

As for the creative powers of the press, Evelyn Waugh gave in "Scoop" a masterly description of one instance when in the beginning was the written word. One fine morning a gifted reporter named

Wenlock Jakes boarded a train en route to one of the Balkan capitals where his editor had sent him to cover a revolution. "He overslept in his carriage, woke up at the wrong station... went straight to a hotel and cabled off a thousand-word story about barricades in the streets, flaming churches, machineguns answering the rattle of his typewriter as he wrote, a dead child like a broken doll spread-eagled in the deserted roadway below the window." In no time, Jakes precipitated a genuine conflict by the sheer eyewitness vigour of his reporting a fictional one.

The conclusion is that unlike God's in Genesis, man's word can create chaos where there was none before.

Impious thoughts on a Good Friday

It is hard to reconcile the detailed narrative of the Resurrection with all its minutiae about who saw the 'risen Christ' when and what was said between them, with the haziness surrounding the ulterior fate of the bodily resurrected Christ

EASTER really brings home Christianity's uniqueness as a religion of Incarnation literally "enfleshing". The Cross, not the crib, is rightly the symbol of Christianity because it is there that "God made flesh" really reveals himself. Paul tries hard, and mostly succeeds, to reconcile the logic and abstraction of Greek philosophy that suffuses Christianity with the claim that Jesus' tortured figure is the vehicle chosen by God to send a message to those he created "in his own image and likeness".

God, Paul explains, does not stand aside while his son suffers endless indignities; he lets this happen on purpose, to show that he takes upon himself the evil, the sin of the world. The Cross is about love of humanity, the outstretched arms of Jesus on the rough and jagged wood are signalling God's embrace of all his creatures. Had the story ended with Jesus' death, Christians could still claim their Saviour's "victory in defeat" thus adding a distinctive ennobling element to their faith.

This, however, is not the end of the story. Christ's death is followed by his Resurrection, his corporeal Resurrection from the dead. All Christian denominations are adamant that whoever thinks that the Resurrection does not concern the body but is spiritual or even worse, symbolic, is not - or is no longer - a Christian.

At this stage one starts becoming a bit confused. According to Christian dogma, Jesus, the Son, is an uncreated divine person like the Father and the Holy Ghost who, together, constitute the Holy Trinity - another feature specific to Christian belief. So is one to believe - pious Christians please stop reading here - that after his Resurrection Jesus rejoined the Holy Trinity, this time in corpore? An "enfleshed" God makes sense as long as he is on earth among his fellow humans, but to think of him as a lonely human member joining an otherwise disembodied Holy Trinity asks too much of the believer.

Let us push the impiety further. A human body has mass, is subject to the force of gravity, is made of tissues and bones; it needs food to eat, water to drink and air to breathe. So the question is: Where has the body of Jesus been for 19 centuries, how has it been catered for and where exactly is it now?

Such questions are easily dismissed by invoking the omnipotence of a God who can do as he pleases without being bound by any constraints. He can, as Blake put it, "hold infinity in the palm of his hand / and eternity in an hour". Plato, infuriated with the stories of deceit, rape and incest of the Greek gods - which he wanted banned - evolved the notion of a "Demiurge" (creator) as the First Cause of everything. However, he insisted that this deity had to respect certain laws. The Christian deity suffers no such limitations except, as some mischief-makers have pointed out, that even God cannot change past history. This God is reached by what Kierkegaard called "a passionate commitment made in objective uncertainty". However, with all the best intentions of the world it is hard to reconcile the detailed narrative of the Resurrection with all its minutiae about who saw the "risen Christ" when and what was said between them, with the haziness surrounding the ulterior fate of the bodily-resurrected Christ. This is what makes some people feel that Easter's imagery of Resurrection and Ascension is archaic and vulnerable to atheist ridicule.

No matter. The fact is that we celebrate Easter anyway. We throw open the windows and let in the sun. In Greece we turn these holy days into memorable holidays. We break eggs and say "Christ is risen." We feel close to our fellow humans and make more use of the word "love" than usual. The other monotheistic religions keep their God strictly spiritual, abstract, austere, demanding, vindictive even. Perhaps Christians could propose to them and also to unbelievers that if commitment to a particular concept of God creates problems, or even becomes a source of conflict, then commitment to goodness, toleration and love - the values that dominate Easter - can appeal to all humans no matter which God - or even if any - they happen to revere.

Does it matter what Jesus looked like?

Without the Resurrection, there is no Christian religion.
One is left only with the teachings of a fallible human

CHRISTIANITY is the only religion in the world that claims we were visited by the incarnate God in the person of Jesus, a historical figure, whose documented crucifixion and reported resurrection is celebrated every year at Easter.

The dual nature of Jesus, Son of God but also "perfect man" free of the Original Sin - only transmitted by the male sperm, as St Augustine explains at some length - is central to Christianity.

This explains why the church resents the prominent nose, the olive skin and the plain, somewhat hirsute image of what Jesus may have looked like, that archaeologists have put forth.

Portraying Jesus as a serene, handsome youth with beautiful pensive eyes and golden hair is important for signalling his divine nature. Any downgrading of his physique risks rendering this incarnate God indistinguishable from other humans, which smacks of heresy.

There was a lively debate in the early church about the dual nature of Jesus. The Nestorians emphasised, during the first half of the 5th century, his humanity. They were condemned as heretics at the Council of Ephesus in AD 431. The Monophysites insisted that Jesus' divine nature had somehow engulfed his humanity. They were in turn condemned at the Council of Chalcedon (AD 451) that elaborated the concept of the double nature (dyophysite) of Jesus Christ. This has been an integral part of Christian dogma ever since.

If Jesus is mainly seen as a human being in all his frailty ("let this cup pass from me" Matt 26:39 and Mark 14:36) and weakness ("My God, why hast thou forsaken me?" Matt 27:46 and Mark 15:36), then at Easter time when his Calvary is evoked and vividly described, it makes a lot of sense to take sides: love this man, loathe Judas, hate the Jews and despise Pilate. The Resurrection, though, then becomes a problem because men, even those who are "perfect", do not rise from the dead.

Without the Resurrection, however, there is no Christian religion. One is left only with the moral teachings of a fallible human martyr who died for what he preached at the hands of brutes, like many before and after him. On the other hand, the Monophysite approach turns the whole Easter story into some kind of charade.

If Jesus did not really become a man in the full sense but merely took on the outward appearance of a man - reminiscent of Zeus who could be transmogrified at will into an eagle or a bull - then Calvary loses all its poignancy, and Jesus' momentary lapses are reduced to play acting.

The "duality" issue is not therefore as esoteric as it sounds and even has unexpected consequences. For two millennia the Jews - who had never crucified anyone while the Romans did so routinely - have been stigmatised as the arch-villains of the story and collectively persecuted as deicides. If you believe in Jesus' dual nature, however, there are good reasons for lifting the curse on those who connived at his crucifixion because by doing so they did play, after all, their part in the divine scheme to save mankind and spread the Christian message of love among humans.

Persecuting people for their beliefs should thus no longer make sense for Christians. Patriarch Vartholomeos certainly thinks so. Other Orthodox leaders in the Balkans seem not so sure.

Should the status of Virgin Mary change?

Contributing to Mariolatry (the worship of Mary) is an increasing frequency of her apparitions that seem to rival those of Elvis Presley in the US

ONCE again pilgrims from all corners of Greece travelled this year, with great hopes, to the island of Tinos to receive the blessing of the Virgin Mary on August 15, the day when all Christians celebrate her Dormition. The Panaghia (All Holy) is popular in Greece. Orthodoxy honours her as a wonderful human being without whom the Incarnation could not have taken place but does not actually worship her, an act due to God alone.

The New Testament is somewhat ambiguous about Mary's views. Unlike Luke who praises her, Mark portrays her as one of the members of Jesus' family who tried to silence him. Jesus himself was no family man, even less a mother's boy. When Mary and his brothers came to speak to him and stood outside a crowded room where he was preaching, he refused to go to them saying: "Who are my mother and my brothers?" And looking around on those who sat about him, he said:

"Here are my mother and my brothers! Whoever does the will of God is my brother and sister and mother." (Mark 3:33-35).

Considering the Panaghia as entirely human, Orthodoxy rejects the Roman Catholic dogma of the Immaculate Conception of Mary by her mother Ann, promulgated by Pope Pius IX as late as 1854.

The Orthodox believe that at the moment of Annunciation on March 25, Mary - as much a descendant of Adam as everybody else - was liberated from original sin by the Holy Spirit and that only Jesus was actually born without original sin. By extending this privilege to the Virgin Mary, the Catholics bring her dangerously close to the Holy Trinity.

Mariolatry (the worship of Mary), although not officially sanctioned by Rome, is nonetheless tolerated and actually spreading in the Catholic world. Contributing to this is an increasing frequency of her apparitions that seem to rival those of Elvis Presley in the US.

Contrasting with her discretion and humility as written in the Gospels, Mary is loquacious and prophetic in her apparitions. She was at her most solemn on May 13, 1917 when she allegedly appeared before children in Fatima, Portugal. The secrets divulged to three little girls are taken most seriously by Rome and the Vatican. Pope John Paul, for instance, is convinced that it was the Virgin of Fatima who rescued him from a Turk's bullet and almost certain death in 1981, on the feast day of "Our Lady of Fatima" as it turned out.

Since then Mariolatry has made great strides in the United States. Even feminists tend to celebrate her as a free woman who chose to make salvation possible by saying "yes" to God at the Annunciation, while Eve had brought about the Fall by saying "no" in the Garden of Eden.

Thousands all over the world have signed a petition to the Pope asking him to name her as the Mediatrix between God and men.

"This is heresy," according to Reverend George G. Parrias, chancellor of the Greek Orthodox Archdiocese of America.

"It is one thing to ask Mary to intercede with her Son, but quite another to exalt her as the Mediatrix between God and men."

As an Anglican theologian put it:

"The Virgin Mary is much displeased by all efforts to increase her status at the expense of that of her Son."